SHOW UP AS *Her*

SHOW UP AS *Her*

10 LAWS FOR RECLAIMING YOUR POWER, EMBODYING MAGNETIC ENERGY, AND POSITIVE MANIFESTATION

CORAL GABLES

For permission requests, please contact the publisher at:
Mango Publishing Group
2850 S Douglas Road, 2nd Floor
Coral Gables, FL 33134 USA
info@mango.bz

For special orders, quantity sales, course adoptions and corporate sales,
please email the publisher at sales@mango.bz. For trade and wholesale
sales, please contact Ingram Publisher Services at customer.service@
ingramcontent.com or +1.800.509.4887.

Show Up as Her: 10 Laws for Reclaiming Your Power, Embodying Magnetic
Energy, and Positive Manifestation

Library of Congress Cataloging-in-Publication number: 2023941727
ISBN: (pb) 978-1-68481-195-3, (e) 978-1-68481-196-0
BISAC category code: OCC014000, BODY, MIND & SPIRIT /
New Thought

To every current and future Positive
B.I.T.C.H. (Babe In True Connection With Herself)—
this book is a tribute to those who are courageously embarking on
the most life-altering revolution of all: reclaiming their own power.
In a world that has taught us to give our power away, may these
pages inspire you to stand unapologetically on your own pedestal.
You are the true revolutionaries, and this book is a testament to
your journey back home to yourself.

CONTENTS

Prologue

Every story starts somewhere, and this is where mine begins.

Date: July 2, 2019
Location: St. Dominic Chapel
Scene: Crying in the middle of an aisle
State of mind: Not okay

Why was I hysterically crying in the middle of a chapel? Well, I was about to head into my senior year of college, and I felt unbelievably lost. I knew I wanted to do something creative, but it felt like I was embarking into the Wild West without any guidance. Why couldn't I just want to be an accountant? You go to school, take a couple of tests, and bam! You're an accountant. But when I thought of doing something "creative," my mind just went blank, except for some ideas that were equivalent to tumbleweeds: dry and fleeting. There were so many options, yet none of them seemed viable. The only thing longer than the name of my double major, TV/Film and Digital Technology/Emerging Media, was the list of things I could do with it. I was able to do *anything*, from being a TV host to being an event planner. You'd think having so many options would allow you to easily choose, but for me, it had the opposite effect.

I felt immense pressure that I was about to graduate and all I had was mental tumbleweeds. What was I supposed to do with mental tumbleweeds? I'm pretty sure you can't put those on a resume. So, what did I do? I did what any fine double-major senior student with no idea where their life was going would do: I had a mental breakdown, duh! My mom, knowing the situation, suggested I try going to the chapel to talk to God and get some answers. I would've flown up to heaven itself if I could get the answers I needed. So, off to the chapel we went.

As soon as I entered, I just lost it. As my mom knelt to pray, I followed suit. Well, I tried to follow suit. I didn't exactly make it all the way into the pew. My version of praying, Praying 2.0, looked a bit different. It included, but was not limited to: flailing arms, millions of tears, sniffles, and repeatedly asking, *Why?* I didn't care who was there. I'm not even sure if there were other people. I collapsed in the middle of the aisle, having what looked like an exorcism. I begged for answers. *God, I don't care what it takes, I need to know what to do with my life. Remove what needs to be removed and clear my path so I can clearly see where to go. I would say I'm about to lose it, but I think I already did that part, so I'm going to need the next steps. Please. Thank you.*

Date: July 5, 2019
Location: Bedroom
Scene: (Still) crying, but this time in my bedroom
State of mind: Beyond batshit crazy

Did I mention I had a boyfriend? Well, a sort of boyfriend. As I questioned my whole entire life, of course I questioned my relationship too. I didn't know who I was or what I wanted. I felt for a while I had to break away and get some space to develop into my own person. Did I think we should break up? Yes. Did I break up with him? Like I said, sort of. I still loved him with my soul—not even my heart, my soul—but I felt unhappy. He was my first love, but I had no love for myself. I had him, but I couldn't find me. He was the sweetest, most loving man, but I was miserable. I knew something was wrong. I just didn't know exactly what it was. We decided on a "break," which turned into a gray-area relationship. You know, like the one in *Friends*, where Rachel and Ross are "together" but also not "together." We still saw each other every weekend, were intimate, and spoke to each other lovey-dovey like we always had. The only difference now was that we could also essentially do what we wanted when we weren't together—we just had to be honest with each other.

"I can get over a lot, but the one thing I cannot forgive is dishonesty. Always be real with me as I am with you," I said.

I don't know if he was daydreaming about the Mets or something, but apparently the honesty part wasn't heard. After spending the Fourth of July in New York City together, we went back to my house on Long Island. While we were in the backyard grilling, his timer for the burgers went off. As I went to click it off, I saw an unfamiliar woman's name pop up on his phone. For the sake of this book, let's call her Liz.

"Who is Liz?" I asked.

Unfortunately, I didn't even need a response. I knew. Even though I was the one who had wanted the break, this was the thing that broke me. For two and a half hours, I questioned him as to who this woman was, but he wouldn't budge and insisted they were friends. I could just see in his face he wasn't telling me the truth.

"Okay, fine, we kissed, but that was it," he said.

"I know you're lying," I responded.

I continued to scream, cry, and question—the triple threat. Suddenly it hit me. In the middle of absolute heartbreak, misery, and anger, there it was. My tears just stopped. I smiled. I started laughing.

"Oh my God. OH MY GOD! OH MY GOD! THE CHAPEL. This is DIVINE INTERVENTION. Oh my God. GOD IS REAL!" I exclaimed.

11

Divine Intervention: When God, or higher-vibrational beings, intercedes in your life, forcing a certain circumstance to push you in another direction. The circumstance will be so synchronistic, you will know it's beyond coincidental.

I had asked God to remove what needed to be removed, and here He was, doing the damn thing! Until July 5, 2019, my gray-area boyfriend and I had never once grilled. He never once set a timer, and I never once just randomly looked at his phone. God was at work here. This was too on-the-nose to be a coincidence. I don't know how much of a believer I was at the time, but this for certain turned me into one. I now have realized I should have been a bit more clear in prayer: *God, remove what needs to be removed, but make sure my heart is not broken in the process.*

Positive Bitch Tip: When you're asking for what you want, be as specific as you can.

"I know what you did. Just say it." I said.

His face fell, and that was my confirmation. They had slept together. He tried to hide it. He did a terrible job at hiding it. I told him to leave. He did. I played "Don't Hurt Yourself" by Beyonce the rest of the night and cried. I felt relieved and destroyed at the same time.

Date: July 6, 2021
Location: Bedroom
Scene: Waking up and remembering it was not a dream
State of mind: Coming to terms with reality

I didn't think it could get worse, but then I woke up the next morning and, to my surprise, it got worse. The night after I found out, I think I was in shock for most of it. That next morning, that is when it hit me. It felt like a dream, but this was my reality. How could this be happening to me? My best friend, the man who is in love with me, who didn't want the break, the one who said he would be honest with me always, who I never worried about—*he* is the one who did this?

The most horrifying part of this whole entire scenario was that I thought I knew him. I spent three years with him. We had spent hours, days, weeks at a time together, yet I never saw this coming. I also thought I could trust myself and that I was a good judge of character. Because of his betrayal, I felt self-betrayal for not knowing better. I knew we had gone on a break, but I'd never thought he would actually sleep with someone else. Not just sleep with someone else, but lie about it to my face. The lie, the timeline, and the denial replayed in my head for what felt like eternity.

My mom would try to literally spoon-feed me oatmeal in the mornings, but I couldn't keep anything down. Oatmeal wasn't going to fill the gaping hole within my body. Nothing would. I was hollow, hurting, and heartbroken. I could barely get oxygen down, let alone a meal. My life and body were going through a spiritual purging.

Spiritual Purging: Process by which the body rids itself of bad energy through various outlets.

Looking back on this period of my life, my heart goes out to my past self. That version of me was barely holding on, and she wasn't sure she would ever find a way out of her own darkness. I'm so proud of her for not giving up. She didn't accomplish everything on her own though. As you will soon see, there were angels put on my path to guide me and support me through my journey. These angels came in the form of therapists, shamans, and healers who offered me love and advice along my way.

My name is CiiCii, by the way. We will get to know each other more in the next chapters. But before that, a quick PSA: Whether you are going through a similar heartbreak, are feeling lost, or just desperately want more for yourself, this book is for you. It is no coincidence that you are reading these words right now. If you've been praying, wishing, or hoping for an answer to change your life, your angels have guided you to this book. It is my hope to pay forward the kind of support I received, as well as offer guidance to help you grow through your own darkness. Oh, and by the way, your darkness is *your* darkness. It's for you to feel, experience, and heal through. It's completely unique to you and not for anyone else to judge. While feeling lost during college and going through a breakup may not seem like a big deal to some, for me it felt like, well, death. This may seem dramatic to a reader, but it really was a death of who I knew myself to be, and it was a tremendous turning point in my life. It's important to acknowledge that everyone goes through different traumatizing struggles, and all of them are valid. While our external circumstances will not look the same, the emotions that we feel— powerlessness, grief, despair, longing, anxiety, and depression—are common for many of us. Let's hold space for each other to feel and heal this shit out together. You don't need to live someone else's life to understand what they're feeling. Many external circumstances can cause the same emotional outcome. Try seeing the commonalities instead of feeling the need to compare. But let's not get ahead of ourselves. Now, where was I? Oh right! Crying!

I cried every single day. I tried to hold onto my life the best I could, but in most moments, I just wanted it to end. I told myself, "Just get through the next twenty minutes," every twenty minutes. I couldn't think about surviving the whole day, because surviving one hour was

14

too painful. This was not a reality I knew how to exist in. How was it possible that, after all of this, I wanted him more than ever before? He was my best friend. Anytime I was upset, or needed a shoulder to lean on, I would go to him. Who was I supposed to go to now? The loneliness crept in.

Date: January 21, 2020
Location: Den
Scene: Movie night with gray-area boyfriend
State of mind: On edge

Gray-area boyfriend and I talked on and off for about six months. I don't know if you have ever experienced a "What are we?" sort of relationship, but take it from me when I say they are not it. Unless you enjoy being a walking question mark, I would stay away. We would see each other, I would get triggered, get upset, and then kick him out, only to miss him and want him back. I couldn't understand nor process what I was feeling because I was still too close to it. One night, after watching a movie, I suddenly felt like he was texting another girl. I lost it yet again and told him to leave. I think the exact words were, "Get out and don't talk to me again." I'm not proud of this version of me. When I think about her, I still hurt for her. When I think about that version of him, I still hurt for him too. We were two hurt individuals who didn't have the tools to move forward together.

Date: January 23, 2020
Location: Kitchen
Scene: Mental breakdown
State of mind: Grief

We didn't talk for a day, and those feelings of needing him were creeping back up, so of course, I snapped at him. He was being cold, so I called him to see what was up.

He said, "You said to get out and not talk to you ever again, so I'm not going to."

I responded, "You do realize this means you can lose me forever, right?"

He responded, "Yes."

I thought I was broken, but this broke me more.

Amid complete destruction, for a moment, I was so numb that I almost felt peace. I had a sudden and supernatural feeling that my brokenness might somehow let the light in, if I could just find the light. I was lost in a deep dark tunnel, but I knew that at the end of each tunnel, there is a light.

Date: March 3, 2020
Location: Parents' bedroom
Scene: Crying, but this time in my parents' bedroom
State of mind: Completely lost

My parents were starting to get tired of watching me deteriorate inside and out. They were concerned that I wasn't getting better. They were frequently staying up with me till three in the morning, watching me weep for hours, listening to me whenever I needed a shoulder to cry on, and holding my hand throughout the whole process. I could distract myself by going out every Friday and Saturday, but the weekdays were awful. Escaping on the weekends seemed to be working less and less. I was getting tired of talking to random guys, drinking, and staying out till five in the morning. God forbid I should see a girl comment on Gray Area's photo while I was doomscrolling in bed at night, because then I would be in shambles.

I sobbed to my parents, "I don't know what's wrong with me. My heart hurts, so, so, so bad. I can't do this anymore."

Knowing I needed help that was beyond my parents' expertise, my mom suggested that I meet with a therapist, Dr. Kay, who I had met before and absolutely loved. There was just something about her that I connected with. I felt like she saw me in ways other therapists didn't seem to. I wiped my tears and agreed. Even though my last adventure with my mom at the chapel had caused a domino effect of unfortunate events, I was willing to give this a shot.

Date: March 5, 2020
Location: Dr. Kay's office
Scene: Therapy session
State of mind: Hope

In the elevator up to Dr. Kay's office, I felt a sense of hopelessness and reached out to my mom like a life raft in a storm.

She combed my hair with her hand and said, "I know, we're going to get you out of this, I promise."

Into Dr. Kay's office we went, and right on cue, the tears started to fall. I explained to her the entirety of the story, and in a matter-of-fact tone she just said, while putting her hand on her heart, "Oh CiiCii, this has nothing to do with him, this has to do with you."

I just stared at her in confusion and thought, *No, lady, I'm pretty sure I am crying about the person who just left my life, NOT ABOUT ME.*

She continued, "This is much bigger than him. He may have triggered this reaction, but he isn't the initial cause of it."

Suddenly my legs went numb, and I got goosebumps. For whatever reason, I was having a strong bodily reaction to her words. My conscious mind could not wrap my head around her words, but my body knew.

"CiiCii, I think you can transcend. Have you ever read the book *The Power of Now*?"

I realize now that this was a critical point in my life. My intense feelings of incompleteness had led me inward. I felt I had a choice to make, and whatever I chose would change my life forever. I could allow my story to continue to tell me, or I could be the one to tell my story. I decided to take back my pen and write my story. So what did I do? I figured I literally could not feel any worse, so why not read what Dr. Kay recommended? If reading that book had even the slightest chance of shifting how I felt, it was a chance worth taking. If reading the book didn't do anything, at least I would have had something to distract me for the time being. I knew I had to try something new, because what I was doing, a.k.a. crying every day all day, wasn't the cure I was looking for. What I didn't know was that reading one book would lead me to spiritually awaken, find my purpose, and lead me back home to myself. While I didn't understand half of what I read, it got me curious. I started looking at myself and the world differently. I started asking different questions which led me to different answers.

As I turned my attention to things other than Mr. Gray Area, I was not only learning interesting new things, but also having waves of positive emotions wash over me every so often. I remember one night specifically when things really took a positive turn. I was standing in front of my mirror, feeling quite unamused at my reflection. My eyes darted from my stomach to my thighs, to my hair, to my skin, to my arms, to my lips, to my...you get the point.

It was so easy to pick apart everything I saw. It was even easier to blame my life, and my reflection, on my past, on the people who had hurt me, on my anxiety, on society, on my genes, even on gluten.

I admit that one was a bit of a stretch, since I wasn't sure if I had any sensitivity, but still, standing there dignified, I thought, "This is probably gluten's fault."

I was angry at life and felt powerless. I saw myself as a victim of circumstance, which is just another way of saying, "Well, there is nothing I can do, so I might stay in this familiar dumpster fire I call my life."

Then my gaze shot back up to eye level, and I found myself looking into my own eyes. There was something intriguing about looking at nothing else but my eyes. I stepped closer to the mirror to investigate the ins and outs of my irises. I turned on my mirror light and marveled at how my pupil constricted itself to allow less light in. Within seconds, my eyes knew how to adjust themselves to keep me protected and healthy. It was then that I realized that my body was working for me. It was always working for me. It was in this exact moment that a flood of information downloaded into my being. This is what many in the spiritual community refer to as a "spiritual download."

Spiritual Download: Spiritual downloads are random bursts of high-vibrational inspiration, guidance, knowledge, or ideas that convey a message to help us along our journey.

I literally gasped. It was like a light bulb went off in my head, and I understood that I was so much more than just this powerless victim. I realized, *If I got myself here, I can get myself out of here too.*

My life circumstances weren't about my ex, my past, or anyone else. My focus, my attention, my thoughts, my energy, my actions, and my habits are what got me there. It was *me*. I was the culprit! **If I kept blaming my life on circumstance, I would never get the power back into my hands.** In taking responsibility over my life, I finally took my power back.

If this was the life I had created by accident, I wondered what kind of life I could create on purpose. This propelled me into action.

The sad sleepless nights I'd once had turned into nights of discovery as I read books, listened to podcasts, learned different spiritual teachings, signed up for seminar after seminar, and talked to God. As I dived into quantum physics, self-love, and manifestation, I noticed that I focused less on my past and more on what I could do with myself now. I would read about a concept and then immediately experiment with it. I didn't want to just learn, but truly understand how I could heal myself and work with the Universe around me. Through my own experiences, I began to understand how to use my power to manipulate the energy around me and create a better life.

Instead of dating my "past" I began to date my "present." I became obsessed with becoming the best version of myself. My spiritual awakening was not a sudden burst of insight; rather, it's an ever-unfolding process of awakening to my own power. I took my power back by taking my focus back and placing it upon subjects that would allow me to grow, rather than subjects I didn't have control over.

Empowerment didn't arrive as a gift on my doorstep; it was something I gained through disciplined focus on myself and my present moment.

As I began to awaken to my own power on the inside, the changes became evident on the outside. Instead of spending my time crying, I now had energy to create. I channeled this newfound energy into starting my own coaching business and podcast, and built a social media following across multiple platforms. I released forty pounds, healed my relationship with my ex, and felt empowered. Before I knew it, I was reaching millions of people globally and helping them become the subjects of their own lives again.

The changes I've made to my mindset, body, career, and love life, as well as the changes I've helped others make in their own lives, are a living testimony to how impactful standing in your own power is. Once I saw myself, as well as my clients and followers, transform, I knew I had to continue to share this knowledge with the world. I have committed myself to a lifetime of learning and teaching about the energetic world unseen.

I am a devout Positive Bitchologist.

My journey from heartbreak to wholeness is an ongoing testament to the power we all have within us, but seem to have forgotten about. If I have the power to drastically change my life, so do you. On some level you know you're meant to stand in your power. A part of you knows you're meant to feel empowered, loved, and whole. If you are giving your power away, it won't feel good. You won't feel fulfilled, you'll be envious, you will feel lost, and you will feel burnt-out, but of course, that is why you are here. Your own inner light brought you to this book and brought you to me.

) **Positive Bitch Tip:** The biggest secret of all is that you have
(the power to become your own living testimony of success.

I have compiled what I've learned into ten laws, so you too have the
opportunity to locate and harness the power that is divinely yours.

My only question to you is, what will you do?

If you want to stay on the timeline you're on, and you are satisfied
with your life, close this book and don't look back.

If you are ready to take back the pen, take back your power, and
quantum-leap to your desired timeline, you have reached your own
critical point.

> **Quantum leap:** Shifting or "jumping" from one energetic timeline
> to another.

The Ten Laws of Positive Bitchology

B.I.T.C.H. stands for Babe In True Connection with Herself/
Human Self.

> **Positive Bitch:** A Babe In True Connection with Herself/Human
> self. The highest-vibrational version of one's self, which is able to
> attract one's desires with ease.

The word *bitch* has long been used against us. If someone used this word towards us, it was considered an insult. I never understood this. I have always had a natural affinity for this word and viewed it as meaning "friend," thus I often called my friends "my fave bitches." For you to fully integrate the Laws of Positive Bitchology, you must see this word as empowering, rather than disempowering. Imagine yourself as your most desired self, living your most desired life. That is the self that is in alignment with Positive Bitch frequency. By doing this, we are alchemizing the energy society has projected onto the word *bitch*, stripping it of any negative energy and infusing it with positive vibration. When you think about being a Positive Bitch, the only thing you will be able to think of is one powerful badass goddess.

I created Positive Bitchology as a way to become her: Your most Positive Bitch self.

> **Positive Bitchology:** "-ology" means the study of. Positive Bitchology stands for the study of becoming a Babe In True Connection with Herself/Human Self.

Showing up as her is an art. It's an ever-evolving process of self-reflection, growth, fun, rebirth, and course correcting. It's a decision you have to make every single day. Showing up as her requires dedication, consistency, and most of all commitment to the version of yourself you wish to experience. She already exists, but you must activate her and choose her daily. Showing up as her is not something you do once. It's a practice. Just like one has to consistently go to the gym to get results, you must consistently decide to tap into her to get the results you want in life. Showing up as her is not about your gender. Rather it's a symbol for the frequency you must broadcast so you can attract the life you want. Showing up as her is choosing to live consciously with the thoughts you're having, the habits you participate in, and the energy you're broadcasting. Showing up as her is a lifestyle that unlocks your desired life.

Each law has a corresponding chapter that will focus on a single area of your life, how you may have given your power away in that area of your life, and how to take your power back. By the end of this book, you will understand how to put these laws into action and embody her , manifesting your dream life.

The Ten Laws of Positive Bitchology gives you a framework to show up as her and get the life you want. They are:

1. Positive Bitches Break Through, Not Down

2. Positive Bitches Are Sexy Because of How They Think, Not Just Because of How They Look

3. Positive Bitches Heal Destructive Patterns, They Don't Repeat Them

4. Positive Bitches Use Their Emotions, They Aren't Used By Them

5. Positive Bitches Rest on Their Pedestal and Attract, They Do Not Chase

6. Positive Bitches Are Magnetic Through Mastery of Their Divine Feminine Energy

7. Positive Bitches Catwalk Their Way Through Change, They Do Not Stagnate

8. Positive Bitches Speak Life Over Their Life, Not Death

9. Positive Bitches Believe Everything Happens For Opportunity

10. Positive Bitches Have Faith

1

Positive Bitches Break Through, Not Down

Taking Your Power Back from Your Ego

Conscious Question: "Who Am I?"

The Ego

If someone were to ask me who I am, I would impulsively say, a daughter, girlfriend, an artist, and a business owner. This is how I view myself. This is the story I tell myself, and others, but that is all it is. A story. Humans are obsessed with stories. We watch stories on TV, read them in books, and tell our own stories to strangers and friends alike. We love stories because they create structure around the outside world, which can feel somewhat unpredictable.

To make life digestible, we create stories, attempting to mold our quantum expansive world into a linear sensible one. The part of us that is constantly narrating internally and trying to make sense of this 3D world is our ego. That bitch cannot be trusted.

> **Positive Bitch Tip:** Just because our ego creates a story about our external reality, that doesn't make that story true; it makes it a story, period.

3D World: Our physical perception of the world we experience daily. Even though all things are made up of energy, we perceive them as having three solid dimensions: height, length, and width.

27

Our ego is what allows us to be human. It anchors us into an identity that keeps us a stagnant character in our story. We aren't just an ego, though. We are both human (ego-based) and divine (soul-connected).

Ego: Who we *think* we are; the identity we created subconsciously to gain love and connection. Our ego's main focus is on human survival.

Sometimes, while we are organizing our world into the chapters of our life story, our inner author, or ego, can run into some trouble with, let's say our editor, the soul. When this happens, it sounds a little like this:

Author (Ego): "This is the worst thing that has ever happened to me."

Editor (Soul): "But what if it's actually the best?"

Author (Ego): "That's so stupid."

Editor (Soul): "Is it?"

Author (Ego): "Yes, this is a total setback."

Editor (Soul): "It looks like a setup to me."

Author (Ego): "CAN YOU SHUT UP? I'M TRYING TO GO TO SLEEP."

Editor (Soul): "I'll come back later."

28

As our egos collect outside-world data, organize it, and write internal stories, our souls will frequently fact-check the details. This tends to cause internal conflict. I call this little fun escapade an Inner World War. While our earth realm has had two physical world wars, we tend to have about two hundred of these Inner World Wars a day. When we are trying to adhere to two different voices, our inner author and inner editor, which are governed by two different laws, it can get very confusing. The ego is governed by fear, and the soul is governed by freedom. We are all badass soldiers, attempting to ease our own internal war while juggling outside stressors such as work, relationships, and family. The thing with an Inner World War is that it cannot be won with fighting words, fear, or violence. To end our Inner World War, we must meet it with calmness, curiosity, and compassion. This allows us to find connection with our authentic energy, which leads us to becoming a positive B.I.T.C.H., Babe In True Connection with Herself.

> **Positive Bitch Tip:** Keep your friends close, and your ego closer. The ego is not some evil villain living rent-free in your head. It's an outdated human safety feature that has become faulty in modern-day society. I like to think of the ego as an Earth Add-On. Part of the deal of being human is that we get this ego. Our ego is how we identify. It holds the story of who we are. It encompasses the lines and boundaries for what we think we can, and cannot, do. It is who we think we are, and who we think we're not. It comprises our values, beliefs, wins, losses, good and bad memories. Every time we say, "I am," we are referring to our ego, not to our actual whole being. While most of us get stuck identifying with the ego, we must remember, we are more than a human safety feature.

Everything in this quantum world is energy. Your lipstick, yoga pants, and favorite fuzzy socks—even though they all look solid, down to their smallest atom—are vibrating particles. Our senses limit us to what we can perceive while on earth. Our mind takes our senses literally which causes us to believe that everything is separate and that there are not enough resources to go around for everyone. Just because we sense something doesn't mean it's fact. When I take out my contacts, everything is blurry. Is it a fact that my boyfriend has a blurry face, or is it that I just don't have my contacts in? My eyesight is limited, which limits my experience. We perceive objects and people as solid when they are, in their truest form, energy. Our limited mind builds our ego, which dictates our reality unless we question the story it is telling us.

By the way, it's probably a good time to mention, you most likely have been here before. Energy cannot be created or destroyed, meaning, once our physical bodies are done on earth, our spiritual body keeps it moving and grooving. We won't always be in human form. We may pass from this lifetime into another, or choose a different realm based on our soul's learned lessons and vibration. Either way, our energy continues on. Our soul spans many lifetimes, but our ego could not handle that information. Let's be honest, most of us are barely hanging on in this lifetime; imagine having to remember that time a thousand years ago when your abusive husband married you just to attain a high position, so you escaped on foot across a river, and traveled three villages over with your baby to create a new life as a woman with few to no rights. I did a past-life regression where I saw three of my past lives under hypnosis, and that was one of the lives I reexperienced. Did I have a many-lives crisis after this realization? Absolutely. Is that the point? No!

Soul/Authentic Energy: The energy we come into the world embodying.

Our ego helps us to identify with the lifetime we are experiencing right now, while our soul remembers all.

Our ego is fear-based, while our soul is loving divinity.

Our ego thinks, and our soul knows.

Our ego is under the illusion of separateness, while our soul knows we are connected to everything.

I've had many clients ask me how to identify their ego vs. their soul, and it's surprisingly quite simple. If the voice inside your head is shit-talking you, it's your ego. If the voice inside your head is loving you, it's your soul. Our ego tends to be loud, and obnoxious. Ever go to karaoke and notice that one drunk person hogging the mic? I mean all night, and won't let anyone else give it a go? When someone else does try to take the mic away, the karaoke hogger gets deeply upset and acts out? Our ego is pretty much like that. Irrational, loves to hear its own voice, soaks up the spotlight, and *hates* to be confronted. If we were to confront our ego, that would essentially mean ego death. The ego can't exist as the ego and keep us in our storyline if we know what it's trying to do.

Positive Bitch Tip: Awareness of the ego dismantles its power over us.

We don't want to kill off our ego entirely, we just want it on our side, working with us, rather than against us. Many people try to escape their ego, but our ego isn't all bad, and it was never meant to hurt us. People who spend their entire life trying to ascend beyond their ego completely miss out on the human experience. We came to Planet Earth to be human, and part of being human is the ego. We came here to work with the ego, not against it and not without it. To focus solely on transcending the ego is in essence escaping being human. Rather than try to kill off our ego, we want to learn how to ground ourselves, regardless of what our ego may be saying. We want to learn how to coexist with our ego, living and knowing it's there, but not letting it control our life. Being able to exist peacefully in our body, ego, and soul is what grounds us and allows us to be our most magnetic self. Knowing we are whole and being able to stand in our wholeness elevates our vibration, regardless of external circumstance. Standing in this wholeness is akin to being magnetic because you are owning all the parts of you, rather than trying to escape half of you. We do not want to chase anything outside of ourselves, but we also don't want to escape anything inside of ourselves either.

Our ego only knows our past, and it's operating from a place of fear rather than freedom. Our ego is hyper-focused on human survival because that is all it thinks we are, just this physical human with this one life. It favors predictable people, places, and circumstances because it thinks that if it knows what to expect, it can keep us safe. This isn't necessarily true, but it is what our ego *thinks*. Having your ego always turned on can cause you to perceive everything as a threat, so it's important that we make a distinction between your ego voice and your soul voice. The more you recognize your constant ego chatter, the less confusion you will have when it comes to determining if what you're feeling is anxiety or an intuitive warning.

Our ancestors needed their ego to help them survive in their very unpredictable lives. If our ancestors gathered berries that ended up being poisonous and making them sick, their ego would collect this data and alert them whenever they saw this type of berry again. The poisonous berries were dangerous, and the ego did its job by keeping our ancestors safe in that scenario. In modern society, our ego isn't going off because we are picking up poisonous berries. It's alerting us 24/7, every time we don't get enough likes on Instagram, whenever we watch tragic events on the news, even when we have a confrontation with a coworker. It thinks that anytime something is threatening our connection to others, or something bad is occurring far away, it's threatening our survival. Our ego is in overdrive, writing our life story into something of a horror story. It's sending SOS signals throughout our bodies daily, thinking we may die, when really, it's reacting to our picture getting only ten likes.

How Our Ego Is Created

We know why our ego is created. It gives us an identity that anchors us into this lifetime and creates a sense of illusionary safety, so we don't completely lose our shit, but how does the creation of the ego happen? My theory is that our ego is formulated in a way that ensures what I believe to be our most primal need, of connection and acceptance, will be met. We are social beings. If we isolate ourselves for an extended period of time, we will start to feel depressed, lonely, and uneasy. This need has been passed down to us from our ancestors and lives in our bodies. Instinctively, we know as infants that to survive we must rely on our "tribe," or as we now say, our parents. Our ancestors needed each other to survive. It was impossible for one man to hunt, pick the berries, know which ones were poisonous, make the clothing, take care of the children, and survive harsh unknown environments on his own. Our ancestors lived with many relatives so that they could work as a team to make sure all were fed, clothed, and protected. If a man decided to go off on his own, it most likely meant death. As we grow, we will mold ourselves to be a version of us that our kin, or family, will accept, love, and/or at least give attention to. If they reject or disown us, it feels like death, because that is what it used to literally mean for our ancestors.

The Beginning Stages of the Ego

When we are babies, it is so easy to get attention. At first, people "oooh" and "aaah" at us for literally doing nothing. We just exist, and everyone is smiling, happy, and joyful. Eventually, however, this attention fades, while our need for connection and affection persists. Knowing we still have this need, we look at what our caregivers respond to and mold ourselves accordingly. It's as if we are investigators, and our parents' words and reactions are the clues we use to build our identity. If we know that crying will get our caregivers' attention, that is what we will do. If we learn that that doesn't work, we will try something else. We continue to look to our caregivers as we grow into toddlers to build upon the data we got as babies and keep sculpting our ego.

We tend to crave one of our caregivers' love more, and this is the relationship that affects us the most deeply. I craved love from my mother the most. My dad worked extremely long hours, so the parent I spent time with the most was my mom. I built a very close relationship with her, and always wanted to be near her. My mom and I did everything together. We worked out together, shopped till we dropped together; she drove me to every after-school activity, made every holiday as special as could be, and allowed my creative side to run wild. She took interest in my interests and supported me in everything I have ever wanted to do. She was, and is, my best friend. Our relationship is beautiful, but even beautiful relationships can have unforeseen side effects.

Growing up, I had two older siblings who were both about ten years older than me and a baby brother who was too young to do anything on his own. My mom was needed all the time in all different places. She was overwhelmed, and I mean, who wouldn't be? There were multiple occasions when my mom threatened to leave, not because of me, but because she was upset with the family in general. Even though she meant she was going to sleep over at my grandma's for the night, this felt extremely disturbing to me. To my child's mind, my mom was abandoning me, forever. Whether she was actually going to leave forever or not didn't matter. The fact I believed it to be true was enough to put my nervous system in a spin. I have a couple of memories of her packing up her bags, which caused me to break out in hysterics each time. The fear of my mom abandoning me

34

stayed with me every day. I never knew which time might be the one when she would leave forever, and so I perceived every moment as a potential chance for abandonment. Whenever there was a family party, I would glue myself to her side so I always knew where she was and she could not, as I thought she would do, escape. When she underwent surgery, I remember having the same fear that this would be the last time I would see her. I knew she had to be put under and I was afraid she was never going to wake back up. God forbid my mom was ever late. My mind would immediately go to the worst possible thoughts of either abandonment or death, but either way, she could be gone forever.

While I was not consciously creating a plan to make my mom stay, I would subconsciously manipulate myself so she would. Whenever I helped my mom with something, she gave me so much love and attention and called me the "can-do" girl. In my child mind, I assumed that if I was the best "can-do" girl there was, she would stay, and so that is who I became. I played varsity tennis, soccer, and lacrosse, practiced kickboxing, and was accepted onto dance teams. I was in a musical theater program outside of school, as well Girl Scouts, student council, and every single advanced class, graduated third in my class in high school, and went on to graduate with the highest honor, summa cum laude, from Fordham University. I frequently volunteered, had a great group of friends, made time to practice piano and vocals after school, and focused my attention on creating my own videos on iMovie late at night.

You would think that, being so busy, I would have no time to worry, but my ego's fears consumed me. Even though my mom was class mom and Girl Scout leader, and took me to all kinds of after-school activities, at my core, I was still constantly scanning for when she might get up and leave. In trying to ensure my mom would "stay," I abandoned much of myself. I wanted to make my mom's life as easy as possible when it came to me. I wanted to prove how worthy I was so she would stay. It was as if I was silently screaming, "Look at me, Mom! You can't leave this! Look what I am giving you." She never said I was responsible for her feeling happy; in fact, *no one* said anything at all was my responsibility. My subconscious acts were an energetic dynamic I took on myself because, at that age, I thought it was the best option. As children, we often try to take our parents' pain away because we know we need them. Many of us become more in tune with their emotions then our own. We will adopt all kinds of different strategies to connect to them and give them our joy, hoping it will outweigh their pain. What I did is not unique.

This isn't to say my dad had no effect on me; he did. My mom was hyper-focused on body image, while my dad was hyper-focused on academic success. I found this to be really stressful because, as the can-do girl, I was trying to do everything and do it perfectly. Academic success came easier to me than "skinniness" did, so I felt like I got my dad's approval easily. While my mom was constantly loving me, hugging me, and spending time with me, I still felt I didn't have her approval.

36

) **Positive Bitch Tip**: What we perceive is occurring always
(outweighs what is *actually* occurring.

Even if my mom did "approve" of me, it didn't matter, because I didn't perceive it in that way. I concluded in my own head that I had to look a certain way for her to accept me completely. If I did not achieve her idea of success, which is to be thin and fit, I did not feel like she could love all of me. While her focus on body image had nothing to do with me, I internalized it anyway, and to be clear, society did not help. I remember my mom telling me that if I had thyroid disease like my dad, I would be able to get a magical pill that would make me skinny.

When I heard this, I thought, "Oh my God, I want thyroid disease."

To this day, I think this has played a role in me getting this disease. You can say it's just in my genes, but I believe I turned the gene on by wishing for it, hoping for it, and therefore manifesting it. I proved to myself that I literally was the can-do girl, and I could do anything, even if that meant getting a disease that would possibly lead to me getting skinny to get my mom to see my worth and stay.

I believe I was able to become the "can-do" girl because the role was not already taken in my family. If my older sister had already been the "can-do" girl and my older brother the "can-do" boy, I might have gone the opposite way and rebelled instead. Negative attention is still attention at the end of the day. Becoming a third "can-do" kid would not have given me a way to distinguish myself and get attention.

Positive Bitch Tip: We will become who we must be to get connection, even if it is a negative connection. Yelling at each other is more connected than not speaking at all.

I knew that identity would deeply connect me to my mom, and so I became the most extreme version of it. Tapping into this version of me was extremely uncomfortable, unbalanced, and stressful. I was living my life according to a story I hated, and I was seeing the negative mental and physical effects of it. The identity of the "can-do" girl is just that, an identity; it's not who I actually am. I'm not just a daughter, girlfriend, can-do girl, content creator... I'm a bomb-ass positive multidimensional bitch having a temporary earthly experience, both human and divine, owning her creative abilities while exploring on Planet Earth. I am the consciousness experiencing this human known as CiiCii.

I am sure you might have had a similar experience growing up. I, as well as you, deserve to get to know our whole selves, not just the limited story we are clinging to as our "truth."

Ego Problems

We give our power away when we live in complete identification with our ego. To become a Positive Bitch, we must locate our soul, and un-identify with our ego self. While we were born with free will, most of us aren't using it, and therefore aren't exercising our power. Even when we think we are using our free will, a lot of the time, we are not. This is why people have midlife crises. They think they are living the life they want, when actually they're living the life they think their parent(s) wanted for them.

To say, "This is just who I am," is the same as saying, "I will eventually have a midlife crisis."

Either you can question the story you are telling yourself now, or your true essence will most likely start to bleed out through negative coping mechanisms like cheating, gambling, addiction, repeatedly aligning with abusive partners, anxiety, depression, and other destructive patterns later. I mean, the choice is yours, choose your adventure!

How to Take Your Power Back from Your Ego

No one can take our power away, but we can willingly give it away. We give away our power when our sense of self comes from outside of ourselves, and when we identify with a story we have created, instead of our authentic selves. Do not blame yourself. You were an innocent child who was trying to survive, and you did what you had to do to get connected. If you didn't adopt this identity to survive, you might have fallen into dangerous coping mechanisms that could've caused grave damage. We can't take back our power if we are blaming ourselves. You did the best you could with what you knew, and you got yourself here, which is the perfect place to be.

Sometimes my clients will tell me, "But I knew better and did it anyway."

) **Positive Bitch Tip:** Knowing better is great, but real power comes with our ability to act better.

Whether you had the knowledge or not, if you were able to do better, you would have done better. We want to thank our identity for getting us this far and release it so that we may go beyond who we think we are.

Let's prime ourselves to unlearn our ego, like we prime our skin for makeup.

> **Say aloud, "With gratitude I release the identity I have created in order to survive to make room for my true essence to shine through."**

We usually don't question our identity when things are running smoothly. I got to a point in my life where I was extremely miserable. I was no longer a girlfriend because I was going through a breakup, I couldn't be the can-do girl anymore because I was burnt-out, and I felt completely lost. The pain of where I was began to outweigh the pleasure of the comfort I got from my ego. I couldn't stand being myself one more second. I decided to rewrite my story. When it comes to our ego, we are either willing to continue writing the same story or we are willing to write a new one. I took back my pen and wrote a bit of a different tale, BECAUSE IT'S MY LIFE and I simply can. Get this. If I am a human and I was able to take my pen back to write my new story, so can you! You are also a human who has the same ability. You too are a powerful co-creator, creating in union with an all-loving energy I call God. You have so much more creative authority than you are giving yourself credit for.

Hit a second pump of that primer and claim a new story.

> ### Scream aloud, "I'm taking back my pen and writing my own damn story because I can!"

Get into it, girl! It's okay to get mad for now, but why just get mad when we can get everything? I'm talking about the dream life, career, relationship... This is just the beginning, this is just the first chapter...literally, but also figuratively for you. There is so much to get excited about, we can't stay mad forever, 'cause, ew! That's just not the vibe of a Positive Bitch.

For a final pump of primer, we are going to have to accept whatever our reality looks like right now. We can't move forward if we are in denial about where we are. I accepted where I was, even though I wasn't proud of it. We are so afraid to reach rock bottom, when rock bottom rocks! If you feel like you are at your lowest point, CONGRATU-FUCKING-LATIONS! You literally cannot go any lower; the only place to go from here is UP! You aren't breaking down; you are breaking open to let the light in, you are breaking the box your ego placed you in, and you are breaking the glass ceiling that seemed impossible to penetrate.

> **Positive Bitch Tip:** This isn't the setback, it's the setup; everything isn't falling apart, it's falling together. This is not the breakdown, this is the breakthrough.

Don't worry if things are messy right now—let them be messy, let yourself be messy, because this isn't your final destination, but a stop along the way.

41

Unlearning Your Ego

To take your power back from the stories your ego lives on, you have to unlearn your current identity to relearn your truth. Having awareness of who you had to be is the first step in learning who you are not. As stated before, our identity is just that, an identity; it is not who we are. We have an ego that gives us an identity, but we also have our soul. We are not just ego, and we are not just soul; we are both human and divine. When we bridge these two concepts together, we are able to get a better picture of who we truly are.

Thinking back to your childhood, ask yourself:

☾ *Which caregiver did I crave love from the most?*

☾ *Who did I have to be in order to be loved by this caregiver?*

☾ *How has that affected me today?*

Practice Stepping into the Unknown Meditation

42

Losing my boyfriend in this 3D realm allowed me to question who I was and look beyond that version of myself. Once we lose our attachments to our current reality, there is nothing else there to remind us of who we "are." In the known, we create more known. It isn't until we take a leap of faith and travel into the unknown that we can create new possibilities. If you keep thinking about the same past, you will not be able to create a different future. If you want to create a new future, you must get connected to yourself and create a new present.

Meditating daily is extremely helpful in detaching from who you *think* you are. You have the power to disconnect from the limitations of time, the people in your external reality, and the things that cause you stress and frustration, but you must shift your focus from the external to the internal to do so. Use the following meditation to aid in practicing non-attachment to your current identity. As you disconnect from your ego self, you will begin to connect to your authentic self. In this meditation you will travel further than you have ever traveled before, deep into the darkness of space, to release and transcend the constraints of your external circumstance.

 The following meditation is also available in audio format, which can be accessed by QR code.

Find a comfortable position, either sitting or lying down. Be sure that your spine is straight, and your legs are uncrossed. Have your palms facing upwards. You can allow your eyes to close gently now, or if you prefer to not close your eyes completely, let your gaze rest downwards, looking at the floor or focusing upon a flame.

Begin by bringing your attention to your breath. Take a few moments to simply observe the natural rhythm of your breath. Notice the gentle rise and fall of your chest, the sensation of the breath flowing in and out of your body.

Now, with more focus, guide yourself to take twenty deep breaths, inhaling through your nose and exhaling through your mouth, to further anchor yourself in the present moment.

Set the intention that with each inhale, you invite more clarity, more self-awareness, and more self-acceptance into your being. With

43

each exhale, you let go of any limitations, self-doubt, or external influences that hinder your connection to your authentic self.

If any worry or thought pops up during this meditation, allow your breath to carry away these external influences, creating a space of total freedom and total peace, knowing that any thought, worry or emotion can be exported through your exhale.

After about twenty breaths, turn your attention to your internal light. Visualize a small, flickering white light flame in the middle of your chest. This flame, radiating love and warmth, begins to grow from the center of your chest. This light represents your inner essence, your divine spark that is always present, no matter what is going on in your external circumstance.

Feel this light expand until your whole entire being is filled with light.

This light begins to expand even further outwards from your body, forming a protective bubble around you. This white light bubble acts as a shield, creating a greater space of tranquility and detachment from the external world.

44

Suddenly you begin to feel the white light bubble lift you off the ground. You allow yourself to be effortlessly transported, floating above the room you began this meditation in. You begin to float above the building or home you reside in. You continuously elevate above your city, your state, being transported through the clouds and blue sky. You continue to soar all the way up to space, where you find yourself among the stars, the moon, and the planets.

As you venture beyond the stars and the galaxy, you gradually enter a realm of complete darkness; embrace this darkness. Acknowledge this darkness as a representation of the unknown limitless possibilities that lie within this space.

In this state of pure being, you're disconnected from the outside world and its influences. It is here that you can begin to truly connect with the divine, with your true self, with your creative abilities, with your emotional compass, and with your inner world.

Allow yourself to simply be present, free from any thoughts, judgments, or attachments.

As you rest further and further into the depths of this darkness, begin to tap into the quantum field that we all reside within. This quantum field is always around us, but not always paid attention to. The quantum field is a realm of infinite energy, possibility, and potential that exists beyond the limitations of our physical reality. It is the fabric from which everything in this Universe is woven. In this quantum realm, there are no boundaries, no restrictions. It is a place where intentions and desires can manifest with ease, where the power of your thoughts and beliefs can shape your reality instantly. The quantum field holds the potential for transformation, healing, and creation beyond what our logical minds can comprehend. Feel the limitless potentiality that vibrates through this realm.

45

As you explore this quantum realm of infinite possibilities, engage with your imagination. Envision what you wish to create and manifest.

What do you wish to see in your reality, and watch as it begins to mold itself from blackness into color and into form?

See yourself living your ideal life, experiencing vibrant health, loving relationships, abundance, success, and spiritual growth.

During this process, you can see what you truly want right in front of your eyes. You can feel it, taste it, touch it, hear it... It's so real, and it's right here in front of you now.

Spend some time creating, exploring, and having fun!

As this meditation draws to a close, express deep gratitude for the time you spent in this sacred space of creation and infinite possibilities. Thank yourself for showing up with positive thoughts, new intentions, and your whole heart. You can begin to place yourself back in the room you began in. Wiggle your toes, wiggle your fingers. You can roll your neck, and when you are ready, you can flutter your eyes open. You have successfully detached from your external triggers and have become a creator of the quantum field.

Cherokee Tale

Many times, what is trapping us in our ego is repeatedly stepping back into the known because that is where we are comfortable. This temporary comfort, however, is what leads us to permanent discomfort, as we stagnate, leaving no room for growth. I would like to end this chapter with an ancient Cherokee tale.

An old Cherokee man was teaching his grandson about life.

"A fight is going on inside me," he said to the boy. "It is a terrible fight, and it is between two wolves. One is evil—he is anger, envy, sorrow, regret, greed, arrogance, self-pity, guilt, resentment, inferiority, lies, false pride, superiority, and ego."

He continued, "The other is good—he is joy, peace, love, hope, serenity, humility, kindness, benevolence, empathy, generosity, truth, compassion, and faith. The same fight is going on inside you—and inside every other person, too."

The grandson thought about it for a minute, and then asked his grandfather, "Which wolf will win?"

The old Cherokee simply replied, "The one you feed."

When going about your day, feed your truth and starve your inauthentic ego-driven fears. You are not your ego; you are the consciousness experiencing this human life. You are the soul that transcends lifetimes. You are a powerful multidimensional creator with unlimited potential. As you move through this life, feed your soul by choosing out of love, rather than reacting out of fear. Start choosing love today, practice again tomorrow, and continue this pattern to anchor in Positive Bitch frequency.

2

Positive Bitches Are Sexy Because of How They Think, Not Just Because of How They Look

Taking Your Power Back from Your Thoughts

Conscious Question: "Is This Thought Serving Me Sexiness or Sadness?"

Thoughts Aren't Monsters, They're Energy

Thoughts, like everything else in this quantum world, are energy. In the physical world, our thoughts show up as neurotransmitters in our brain. We think we have no control over our thoughts, but I am here to tell you that you are more powerful than an electrochemical reaction happening in your brain. Just because there are some rusty dusty reactions occurring in your brain, which you perceive as thoughts, does not mean you have to believe those thoughts. Thoughts are just thoughts. They are not objective truths. When we believe every thought, it's like going to a horror movie and thinking the movie is real, falling for every jump scare because you have mistaken it for your reality. We realistically know movies are nothing to fear, because they are just scenes appearing on a screen. We need to apply the same mindset to our thoughts. Thoughts are nothing to fear, because they too are just scenes but appearing on our internal screen. Positive and negative thoughts are bound to cross our mind, but they cannot control us if we remember they're part of a mental movie, not necessarily our reality.

Where Thoughts Come From

We came into the world as loving, confident babies. We were not born with negative thoughts wired into our brains or with self-esteem issues. We weren't embarrassed when someone had to change our diaper and we didn't come out of the womb hating ourselves. When we were in a room, we demanded attention and would cry until we got some. We were born knowing we were inherently worthy of this lifetime just by being born. This means any thought that deviates from confidence, love, or joy is not something we were born with; it is simply something we learned while on Planet Earth.

Positive Bitch Tip: We are not our thoughts. We think thoughts. We experience thoughts. We even receive thoughts, but we ourselves are not our thoughts.

Our ego influences most of our thoughts, which influence our actions, which influence our reality. I believed I was the "can-do" girl, so I thought as a "can-do" girl would think, which influenced me to act as a "can-do" girl would act.

Let's say my mom needed me to help her volunteer, but I wanted to go hang out with my friends. If she asked me for help, my thought would be, *I want to hang out with my friends, but I am the can-do girl, and she needs me.*

This thought would lead me to help my mom without a fuss, rather than follow my authentic desire of seeing my friends. This is how our ego influences our thoughts, actions, and then our reality.

I knew that when I showed up, she would say, "Thank you CiiCii! I knew you would come because you are my can-do girl!"

50

Our ego loves to confirm what it already thinks, which is why we act according to our identity, rather than our authentic self. The more we hear something about ourselves, especially between ages two and six, when our brains are often in theta waves, the more we believe it.

Theta Waves: The brain mainly operates in theta waves when we are toddlers (ages about 2–7). As adults, our brains only operate in theta waves just before falling asleep, right upon waking, while in deep meditation, or when under hypnosis. When we are in a theta state, our subconscious mind is accessible, meaning we are highly susceptible to programming.

The more our parents tell us we are smart, the more we believe them. This is even stronger if our parents talk about us to another person in front of us. If my mom were to say to another parent how much of a can-do girl I was, this wired my identity in even further.

> **Positive Bitch Tip:** They say to believe people when they tell you who they are, but I say, listen up when someone tries to tell YOU who YOU are, because they just may be projecting! Think about the words you heard about yourself growing up. As children, we were vulnerable to the adults around us because we saw them as authoritative figures. We thought that they knew it all. If an adult told us that babies were carried by storks, we believed them. If an adult told us we weren't good enough, we believed them. The voice in our head that tells us we aren't good enough mimics the voice of the person who criticized us the most growing up.

People don't have to say exact words for us to draw a conclusion based on their actions.

If we went to the toy store and our mother told us we weren't allowed to get the newest Barbie doll, she may have said that to be financially smart, but all we may have heard is, "You are not worthy of this toy."

Our parent could yell at us for running in the street for our own safety, but all we got from that is, "You are a bad girl."

A friend could have said she couldn't hang out one day, but the conclusion we came to was, "No one wants to hang out with me."

We were children living in an adult world, so our conclusions didn't always align with the other person's intention. They could mean

51

something completely different, but how we perceive their words and actions is all that matters. Our perception is our reality.

This may be a hard pill to swallow, but it's better to swallow now than choke later. Bear with me here. We can also pick up thoughts through lower-vibrational entities. This is nothing to be afraid of, considering that you've already been doing it; now, you will just have more power over the situation, so if anything, this is a big-ass high-vibe celebration! When we engage in lower-vibrational thoughts, we create an opening for lower-vibrational entities to attach onto us. When a low-vibe entity is a vibrational match for our lower-vibrational thought, that is how they're able to connect to us. It's as if the negative thought is the invitation for the negative entity to party in our energetic field. It's not necessarily that these negative entities want to hurt you, it's just that they are attracted to vibrational matches. When the negative entities attach onto us, they can raise the volume on our negative thoughts, which can cause us to spiral. If you have a thought you cannot shake, like, "I'm not good enough," and it continues to get worse—"I'll never be good enough," "Others are more deserving," "I shouldn't even try," "My life isn't worth living,"—these may not be self-generated, but attracted via negative entities.

Your Thoughts Are Showing

Our thoughts may be held in the private space of our own minds, but they are felt in the public space of the quantum field. Someone does not need to be a mind reader to tell when we are feeling happy or sad. Someone can look at another and see the emotional state they're in based on body language alone. This is because our thoughts affect how we physically show up in the world.

Every single thought we have creates a biochemical reaction in our body. If you have ever been nervous about an interview, an audition, or even a date, you may have noticed your palms began to get clammy, or a sudden stomachache developed. Our thoughts are in direct communication with our body 24/7, and our thoughts aren't shy about telling our body how to feel. Thinking fearful thoughts will cause our body to slip into a fearful state. This brings us to the Resting Bitch Face phenomena. Having a "smug" look on your face, or "RBF," is not just the way your face is constructed. If you are having negative thoughts at the bar, your body will show this. If you are thinking that you are unlovable, your friends are prettier than you, and no one will like you, this will affect how you show up. If you convince yourself that your human connections are being threatened, your body will shift from the parasympathetic nervous system, or rest-and-digest, into the sympathetic nervous system, or fight-or-flight.

Parasympathetic Nervous System: The part of the autonomic nervous system that is responsible for relaxing the body. It's often referred to as "rest and digest" because in this state, we are able to digest properly, conserve energy, breathe deeply, engage with others, and feel safe.

Sympathetic Nervous System: The part of the autonomic nervous system that is responsible for our response to perceived stress. It's often referred to as "fight or flight," because in this state our heart beats faster, our jaw tightens, our body becomes contracted, and we become hypervigilant toward the perceived threat.

When we shift into the sympathetic nervous system because our mind is telling us we aren't worthy of connection, our facial muscles tighten, our body language becomes closed off, and we will scan for potential threats. It's harder to engage with other people when our body is throwing around SOS signals. Our capacity to engage in conversations will start to slow or shut down completely.

Let's break this down.

1. You look into the mirror and think: "I look terrible in this outfit."

At this point, you only have had one negative thought, and you can still turn the night around by refocusing on something else. Your body can still stay in the parasympathetic nervous system.

2. You get to your friend's house and think, "All my friends have so much going for them."

Feeling as if your friends are better than you can cause you to feel like your ability to connect to potential mates is now threatened. Your body will begin to become increasingly stressed. Some symptoms may occur, like headaches or just a general bad mood. You may now begin to shift into the sympathetic nervous system as your thoughts trigger SOS signals to be sent throughout your body.

3. You get to the bar and think, "No one is going to talk to me."

Resting bitch face is officially brewing. As you continuously think fear-based thoughts, your body increasingly becomes ready to fight or flight, tensing your muscles and influencing you to want to socially shut off. Put it this way: you aren't going to look like a happy camper.

4. You're fifteen minutes into being at the bar, and you think: "I knew no one would come up to me."

Resting bitch face takes full effect. Negative thoughts are spewing, you may be very uncomfortable, anxiety may be high, and this can cause you to either start a fight or start drawing up mental escape plans.

If you had a friend who was always negative, you wouldn't feel good around them. When we are always negative in our own head, it doesn't feel good to be in our own skin. We give our power away when we let our mind run wild. We must start taking accountability and responsibility for the thoughts that we are allowing our mind to have on replay. Yes, we will have a negative thought here and there, but that isn't the problem. The problem is that, after the initial negative thought, we are creating ten more negative thoughts which are sending us spiraling.

I invite you to start imagining that your negative thoughts about yourself are no longer private, but instead are a necklace someone gifted you. Now, that's a real statement piece, if you ask me. Imagine that the negative thought "Nobody likes me" has solidified into a physical silver necklace. It's heavy and weighs upon your neck every day. You look into the mirror daily and see this "Nobody likes me" necklace, and everywhere you go, everyone can see how you are thinking about yourself too. Every day you are reminding yourself of the same negative thought, and every day you are strengthening that thought. Eventually, the fake silver from the necklace starts to turn your skin green, you begin to have a neck ache because it's so heavy, and it doesn't even look good with any of your outfits, so what would you do? You would take off the necklace and return it.

We do not need to hold onto projections from others, or thoughts that are no longer serving us. They are not ours to carry. We do not own them. We can take them off and return them to the gifter. If our thoughts were physical jewelry pieces, we would be much more concerned with them. We wouldn't want to lug around that heavy necklace; we wouldn't want to look at it daily, or show other people the truth of what we think about ourselves. We think that, because something isn't physical, it doesn't have a negative impact on us. Sometimes we try to forget about it altogether, but these thoughts are weighing us down. Being in denial that you have negative thoughts will not allow you to transcend to a positive mindset. We don't have to go down because of our thoughts; we have to put our thoughts down.

We are so focused on the 3D, focused on shaping our bodies, we have forgotten to shape our minds, which are influencing our whole reality. Our thoughts affect how people perceive us, not just bodily, but energetically too. We all have met someone who was "stereotypically" good-looking, but because of their energy, we didn't find them attractive, or something was just "off." On paper, they're great, but in person...not so much. Then there are other people who aren't our usual "type," but we have found them attractive. What's this all about? Not only does our body communicate what's held in our minds, our energy talks for us the second we step into a room.

56

Sexiness Is a Mindset

I can go pretty much anywhere, and I will have all kinds of people coming up to me, complimenting me, and telling me they love my energy. This wasn't always my reality, though. I didn't look any different physically, but when I began to shift how I felt about myself, and interrupt the negative thoughts I was thinking, my reality shifted too. I noticed that when I hated my outfit, or felt bloated, my thoughts were extremely negative, which would cause me to be shut-off to others. When I started to tell myself that I am proud of myself, I radiate confidence, and I am super sexy, other people started to see me in that light too. When I told myself these things, my body was able to relax. I walked into every room with a huge smile, with my shoulders back, and felt safe enough to say hello to everyone. My thoughts allowed me to be in the parasympathetic nervous system, because I wasn't telling myself that my connection to others was being threatened.

We are the voice we hear the most, so we must start cultivating a voice that leads us to better feeling places instead of digging ourselves into a hole. Refer to the image below to see how our negative thoughts can completely change our outer expression.

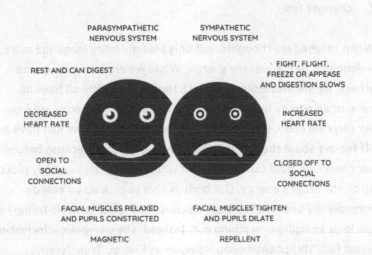

PARASYMPATHETIC NERVOUS SYSTEM	SYMPATHETIC NERVOUS SYSTEM
REST AND CAN DIGEST	FIGHT, FLIGHT, FREEZE OR APPEASE AND DIGESTION SLOWS
DECREASED HEART RATE	INCREASED HEART RATE
OPEN TO SOCIAL CONNECTIONS	CLOSED OFF TO SOCIAL CONNECTIONS
FACIAL MUSCLES RELAXED AND PUPILS CONSTRICTED	FACIAL MUSCLES TIGHTEN AND PUPILS DILATE
MAGNETIC	REPELLENT

Positive Bitch Tip: Sexiness is born in our mind and expressed through our bodies.

When we think about ourselves as being sexy, attractive, and likable, our body begins to rest, which brightens up our external appearance. Not only do we feel better about ourselves, we look better. Knowing you got it goin' on is what increases your magnetic energy and pulls people toward you. When in this state, you signal through your smile and relaxed shoulders that others can and should approach you. Your positive thoughts manifest through your body language and convey that you are open to communicating with others. However, when we stress that we aren't attractive, or think we suck at flirting, we begin to constrict our bodies, which has the opposite effect and signals others not to approach us.

> **Positive Bitch Tip:** If you're not feeling sexy, before you look in the mirror, look inward instead. Your sexiness is accessed through your brain. Your mood, your perception, and your day will drastically change when your mindset changes first.

When I shifted my thoughts, not only was my body language more welcoming, but so was my energy. While we are interacting with others, we are also interacting with their energy. We all have an aura, or an energy field that extends a couple of feet outward from our physical body. If we meet someone at a bar, and we just have an off feeling about them, but don't know why, this is because before our conscious mind can understand what's going on, our body picks up on the other's energy. Our body is able to pick up on energy immediately because there are no conscious mind controls trying to use logic to figure everything out. Instead, the energetic information is just felt. This phenomenon is known as Energy Transference.

Energy Transference: The process in which we exchange energetic information subconsciously when talking or being intimate with others.

People can fake being happy, and even appear to be in a high-vibrational state, but this facade does not last long. When we try to make our body do something different from our mind, we will be able to achieve this, but only for short periods of time. If we try to fake it till we make it, there is one problem. While we are trying to convince everyone around us about who we are, we forget to convince the most important person of all: ourselves. Faking it till you make it does not work long-term because it's trying to make changes only in the 3D. If you want to make a real shift, it must be done internally. Shifting is not about telling others who we are; rather, it's about convincing our subconscious mind of who we are.

The Conscious and Subconscious

We have both a conscious and a subconscious mind. Imagine an iceberg. If you've ever seen an iceberg, you might know that only the tip of it can be seen, while most of the mass is below the waterline. The conscious mind is like the tip of the iceberg—it can be seen consciously, and we know it's there. The subconscious mind is like the mass below the waterline. While we cannot see the bulk of the iceberg, that does not mean it is not there; it just means we aren't conscious of it.

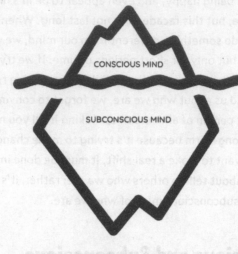

CONSCIOUS MIND

SUBCONSCIOUS MIND

The conscious mind involves everything we know, remember, and are aware of. This can include thoughts we know we are having or memories we can recall. It is useful for reasoning, planning, and deciding. The subconscious mind stores information that is out of our conscious awareness. Our subconscious acts by way of impulses from past thoughts and feelings, rather than using reason. We do not know what is in our subconscious mind, as it is not in our awareness consciously, but that information does still live within us, and can be accessed when we slow down and create room for it to come through.

If you have ever said, "I don't know why I keep doing this to myself," or "I don't know why I am reacting in this way," that is because the root of that behavior is stored in your subconscious mind, keeping your conscious mind in the dark.

Every time I went dress shopping or had to get a costume for dancing school, I always felt this overwhelming stress come over me. I didn't understand this feeling, but I knew I hated it. I felt uglier than everyone else, and out of place. I decided it was time to understand why. I did a deep meditation for forty-five minutes with the intention of understanding this feeling. About thirty minutes into the meditation, I recalled a memory of a performance at my elementary school. It felt like this memory dropped out of the sky into my head. My six friends and I were all going to wear the same type of jeans. When we went to try them on, the jeans fit everyone but me. I was so embarrassed. I just said I didn't like them because I didn't want to say they were too small. One of the moms was visibly annoyed that I didn't like the jeans. I could tell she thought I was being difficult. This made me feel like I was not worthy to be in the performance. This memory was stored within me and deeply affected how I felt about myself when I had to try on new clothes, and I wasn't even aware it was there at all until I quieted my mind and searched for the root.

Manifesting from Your Thoughts

The more we think a thought, the easier it is to think it again. That is how we humans operate. As much as we are multidimensional beings, our human bodies operate like machines. Our bodies learn based on repetition. I may not be the best at playing the piano the first time I sit down, but the more I practice playing the piano, the better I will be. At first, my brain didn't have any neurological pathways in relation to the piano, but as I practiced, the neurons in my brain began to hook up and create something called a neurological pathway. The more I practice, the stronger that neurological pathway becomes.

While we are not our thoughts, we can become them. Anything we consistently repeat, we get better at. We can become so good at repeating a thought that we mistake it for our truth. Once we mistake it for our truth, we give our power away and believe the thought, identify with the thought, and become the thought. If I keep repeating the thought, "I am unlovable," this will become a belief which will bleed into my reality, showing up in my experiences with others. Someone could turn me down because our values don't align, but if I think I am unlovable, I will tell myself that that is the reason for the rejection. What was once a thought, now becomes a belief. The more I tell myself this, the more I wire it in. The more I wire it in, the more I am going to perceive it in my reality. While I was not the thought, "I am unlovable," I was able to become it by consistently telling myself this lie, reminding myself of the lie, molding situations to fit the lie, and then eventually manifesting the lie.

Positive Bitch Tip: When you shift your thoughts, you shift your life. Our mind is like a magnifying glass; what we think about will be magnified in our reality. If I think I am unlovable, I am going to start to see this in every situation, even if no one else is intending for me to feel that way. Think about it like this. If I think all men are trash, I can go to a bar where there are a hundred men, eighty good men, and still align with a man I deem "trash," because my mind is magnifying what I already think and then confirming my thought through my reality. Our mind will magnify the guy who isn't the healthiest for us, and our energy will sniff out their low vibration, leading us straight into the ego trap of confirming what we already believe. We are all always creating; however, some of us aren't creating in ways that are conducive to our desires. Instead, we are letting our negative thoughts be the foundation of our manifestations.

Our dominant thoughts and feelings, whether those are conscious for us or not, create our energetic signature.

Energetic Signature: Every human has an energetic signature. Our energetic signature is made up of our dominant thoughts and feelings, including both conscious and subconscious programs. It's our unique "magnet" that attracts all we experience.

You are always attracting people, places, experiences, and opportunities into your life based on your own energetic signature. I like to think of our energetic signature as our own unique "magnet." Just like each one of us has unique DNA, we each also have a unique energetic signature. You don't have to worry about one negative thought here and there. We have all thought outrageous things, and those things never appeared in our 3D reality. It's not that every single thought and every single feeling manifests, but rather, the thoughts and feelings that are a part of our daily lives will impact our energetic signature. We exist within a quantum field that holds unlimited possibilities or potentials. You turn on possibilities when you feed a possibility with your energy, both mind and heart. The more we think a thought, the more we feed that thought energy until it solidifies into the 3D field. When you feed a thought enough, and give it enough heart, you align with it. If you begin to change your thoughts, which will begin to change your feelings, your energetic signature will change too, which will change your reality. Changes in our outer reality begin in our inner reality.

How to Take Your Power Back from Your Thoughts

To take our power back from our thoughts, we must stop believing that every single one of them is true. I can think that elephants are pink, but that doesn't make it true. We must stop believing that, just because we have a thought, it is the law. There was a time in my life when I deeply feared abandonment, not by my mother, but by Mr. Boyfriend. Oh, the fear of abandonment. This is one fear I would get to know very well. Anyway, I thought that, if he left me, I would absolutely die, and my life would be ruined. Eventually, that biggest fear came true, and guess what bitch made it out alive? ME! When my utmost biggest fear ended up manifesting into my reality, it turned out to be the best thing that had ever happened to me. I thought if that were to happen, it would ruin me, but it was the thing that made me. The thing I feared the most was the thing I am also most thankful for. I found that the things I have feared in my past, when they did happen to manifest, they made me stronger. They were informative. They offered me insight into how capable I really was.

I've had a lot of my clients tell me their fears, and when I asked them, "What's the worst that can happen?" their answers ranged from "I'll be embarrassed," to "I don't know how I would handle it."

My next question was, "Will it kill you?"

Their answers were always no. If the answer is no, you can 100 percent get through it. It might not always be easy, but it is possible, and all we need it to be is possible. We think our worst fears are going to absolutely kill us, end us, beat us, when really, they are invitations to grow.

❤ *Instead of wasting your time spiraling, start asking yourself, "Will this kill me?"*

If the answer is no, LET IT GO. If you are having spiraling thoughts about going on a date or an interview, instead of wasting time picking more low-vibrational thoughts, spend time preparing. In high school, instead of engaging in conversations about how everyone was so afraid of the upcoming exam, I just spent my time studying. Time is a nonrenewable resource; use it wisely.

❤ *If you are having negative thoughts about a specific situation, before you spiral, ask yourself, "Is there something I can do to make myself more comfortable in this situation?"*

Maybe it's spending an extra hour studying, looking into the business you're interviewing for, or even FaceTiming the guy you're talking to before seeing him in person. Many times, there are ways to subdue our anxious thoughts, but instead of taking charge, we allow our thoughts to take charge of us. Instead of feeding the anxious wolf, starve him, and look for solutions. We may not be in control of every single thought we have, but if we are aware that we've had one negative thought, we can guide ourselves to a better second thought.

Not Falling for the Mental Movie

Keep your mind accountable. You know that your thoughts can vary
in truthfulness, so don't give your thoughts the power to ruin your
day. Our perception is our reality, but our perception isn't always
objectively true. This is why there are multiple eyewitnesses. One
event can happen, yet people can view the same event in completely
different ways. We all have a past that affects how we see our
present. The reality we perceive is filtered through who we are, our
beliefs, our thoughts, our emotions, and our experiences. We do
not see things exactly as they are; rather, we see things as who we
think we are.

💜 *Next time you have a thought that doesn't feel great, take
a moment to practice mindfulness and ask yourself, "Is this
thought serving me sexiness or sadness?"*

A thought is serving sexiness if it makes you feel good, happy, joyful,
thankful, or excited, and it is a thought that will help you grow. A
thought is serving sadness if it makes you feel depressed, anxious,
or alone, or is a thought that makes you feel stuck. If a thought
isn't aiding in your growth, it's pushing you toward stagnation. If a
thought is serving sadness, let it go. If a thought isn't helping you,
don't help it exist in your mind by giving your precious energy to it.

💜 *Instead, ask yourself, "What would be a sexy thought?"*

Maybe being a successful CEO of your own company, finding your
soulmate, or moving to a different country. If you want to harp on
something, harp on that SEXY!

Accessing Your Subconscious Mind

Pick a thought or feeling you wish to understand. For example, I picked the feeling of unworthiness and embarrassment when trying on clothes. Close your eyes. Think the thought or feel the feeling that you are trying to gain information about from your subconscious mind.

> ♥ *Ask this thought or feeling, "When did I first experience you?" and allow your subconscious mind to search and find the root.*

This allows you to access your subconscious and understand why you may be experiencing this thought or feeling still to this day. Sit with this for at least ten minutes in a quiet spot, or until you receive an answer. You can also journal about what information you pick up. The information could be in the form of a memory, vision, or sound. Don't try to understand it at first, just allow yourself to be open. Once you receive the information, and have written it down, you can use logic to understand it.

Inviting Your Conscious Mind to the Party

It's important to question your beliefs in order to manifest consciously. When it comes to manifestation, you need both your thoughts and your feelings to be on the same page. If, in my heart, I want to be a famous singer, but in my head I'm afraid to be seen, my reality will not know what to produce in front of me. To become a Positive B.I.T.C.H., you must start questioning your own thoughts, which over time become beliefs. You must make space for your conscious mind to think rationally, rather than have your subconscious mind run the show.

Think consciously about the different spheres of your life:

Love   Money

Friends   Health

Family   Home

Relationships   Career

Write down all your thoughts/beliefs related to each subject. Only when you ask yourself what you think about each subject will you start to identify your limiting beliefs.

> **Limiting Belief:** A limiting belief is a belief that keeps you from growing or getting to the next level in some area of your life. Limiting beliefs keep us in our comfort zone, so our ego loves them, but they ultimately inhibit us from reaching our full potential. They are not based on facts, but on fear.

If I think that the people I love always leave, it will cause me to reject potential partners, abandon relationships, and sabotage love. This belief will not only manifest as truth in my life, it will also keep me in my comfort zone of being single. You can either test your beliefs or go home every night alone and cuddle the limiting beliefs that are stunting your growth. Everything is a choice.

Some common limiting beliefs are:

I'm not good enough

I am not worthy of love

I'll never find a partner

People don't like having me around

You must work extremely hard for money

Rich people are greedy

I have no control over my health

I cannot afford my desires

I am not smart enough

I don't deserve to
be successful

I don't have
enough experience

I am not attractive

I am not likable

No one wants to flirt with me

I am not sexy enough

Once you have identified a thought, you can use my 4R System. The 4R System stands for Recognize, Reduce, Rewire, and Reclaim.

Recognize

We cannot change a thought if we have no idea we are even experiencing that thought. Now that you have listed out some of your thoughts/beliefs, they are coming into conscious awareness. Awareness is the first step to healing anything. You now know what to look for when it comes to limiting beliefs. They are on your radar, and therefore they will be more easily found.

You may be about to go on a date, and you hear yourself say, "Ugh, no one is ever going to love me."

As soon as you hear that thought, recognize her for what she is, a limiting belief! Cue the conscious conversation. Instead of criticizing yourself further for calling yourself unlovable, celebrate that you are gaining conscious awareness of your thoughts. This is big! Even though these may be your thoughts, they aren't your original creations. Depersonalizing my thoughts has helped me stop identifying with them. I am not the thought or the creator of the thought; I am the one experiencing the thought. Instead of aligning with the thought, I observe it. The more you interrupt these neurological pathways, the weaker they will become. Eventually, if these neurological pathways become weak enough, the brain will clear them away. This makes room for new neurological pathways to form. This process of clearing and creating neurological pathways is called neuroplasticity. To put it simply, neuroplasticity makes it possible for our brain to change older pathways and create new ones.

Growing up, my mom always told me, "Negative thoughts are not from God."

She was onto something, as negative entities can stir up negative thoughts within us. Whether you call the ego's voice in your head "the devil" or "Karen" doesn't matter; what matters is that you realize it isn't you. When you stop identifying with your thoughts, you can be like a fisherman. If a fisherman doesn't want to keep a fish, he doesn't take the fish home, cook it, and eat it. He just throws it back in the water, and lets the fish go. Do the same with your thoughts. If you don't like the thought, you don't have to take it home with you, nurture it, and feed it by focusing your attention on it. Rather than absorb the thought, observe the thought.

71

If a thought seems relentless, I invite you to release the energy of it. Just as the ego doesn't like to be called out, negative entities do not favor it either, so when it comes to removing these energies, we do it with grace.

First, ask, "Is there a spirit here?"

If you hear, feel, or have a knowing it is a yes, then ask, "Are you from the light?"

If it's a yes, you can simply have gratitude for this being supporting you; if it's a no, you will want to inquire further.

Ask, "How have I attracted you?" and/or "Why are you here?"

I like to do this so I can understand why I've attracted and lived with a certain darkness. I once had a spirit tell me it added to my thoughts of not feeling good enough to keep me "safe" from being seen. At this time, I had a fear of being seen. It's not that this energy was evil; it was attracted to my like vibration and added more of

that low vibration which kept me stagnant. It offered me comfort, but ultimately, I wanted more.

Next, with love, send this energy to the light. I like to ask my spirit guides, which we will talk about in later chapters, for help.

Say, "Highest in vibration, healing spirit guides, help me in releasing this spirit to the light."

Speaking directly to the low-vibe entity, "With love, I release the spirit that made me think _____. Go gracefully into God's white light, where you will be embraced In unconditional support. Rest in the light where you will gain eternal love."

After this, I will wait for confirmation from my spirit guides that the process has been completed. If not, repeat the statement above. If it is completed, I thank the spirit, my spirit guides, and God, for this lesson and my leveling up.

Reduce

Once we recognize that the thought is occurring within us, but is not from us, we can begin to reduce it. Instead of bringing criticism to our party, we want to invite curiosity.

Ask yourself:

☾ *Why do I believe this?*

☾ *Who told me this was true?*

☾ *Have I ever actually seen this to be true?*

☾ *What am I getting from this belief?*

☾ *Do I like what I am getting from this belief?*

☾ *Don't I want more than what this belief has to offer me?*

☾ *How much longer can I keep this belief up?*

☾ *What are examples of this belief being false?*

Reducing the belief allows you to see that this belief is simply a statement you came to believe was true by repeatedly thinking about it. Repeatedly thinking about it causes it to affect your energetic signature, which in turn manifests circumstances of similar vibration to show up in your life. While you may have seen it in your reality, it is because of your signature, not because it is objectively true for everyone.

72

Rewire

Our subconscious mind is programmed by our conscious mind. This makes our subconscious mind very vulnerable, because it believes whatever we tell it. If I keep telling my subconscious mind that I do not deserve good things, my subconscious mind will believe me. What we tell ourselves consciously will be believed by our subconscious mind and stored in our body. While we are not our thoughts, we can become them if we create a habit of thinking them.

It's hard to jump from a negative thought to a positive one immediately. If we are in a very low vibration, lower-vibrational thoughts may be the only ones in vibrational reach. To be able to reach for positive thoughts without frustration, we will want to take a pause to bridge ourselves to a more neutral or positive mindset. Take an inhale through your nose and exhale through your mouth to change up your chemistry further. You're ready to rewire. Say a positive statement that is in opposition with your original limiting belief.

If the belief was, "I am not enough," the opposite positive affirmation would be, "I am more than enough."

I recommend writing a list of these positive affirmations somewhere— it can be on your mirror, on sticky notes, or in a notebook—so that you have a personalized list of positive affirmations. If saying a positive affirmation feels false, find a neutral statement instead.

If saying, "I am more than enough" feels phony, say, "I am working on myself every day."

We are not policing our thoughts, but rather guiding them to a more positive place via baby steps. Over time, baby steps build to big steps.

Reclaim

It's time to reclaim your crown. Invite movement into the process, either by putting your hands on your hips like Superwoman, shaking your hips, or making whatever movement feels powerful for you.

Say, "I am (insert your name) and I am going to live as I want."

Positively spiral about how you are creating the life of your dreams. Have fun with this part. You are reclaiming, rebirthing, and resetting. You are taking your power back from your thoughts and taking control of your life. You are claiming your inherent right as the creator of your own reality.

3

Positive Bitches Heal Harmful Patterns, They Don't Repeat Them

Taking Your Power Back from Your Past

Conscious Question: "Is This in Alignment with Who I Am, or Who I Was?"

The Map Behind the Pattern

When our soul decided to incarnate as a human on this planet, part of the deal was that we would forget all that occurred before. When we are born, we must learn how to operate as a human on earth. Our caregivers had to teach us how to walk, talk, attach to others, be in relationships, react to external circumstances, and behave. Our caregivers essentially taught us how to be human. What they didn't outwardly teach us, they showed us through their own behaviors, which we subconsciously noted and internalized. While growing up and learning from our caregivers externally, we were simultaneously internally creating "maps," tracking what we learned.

If we saw our caregivers kissing and hugging, we thought, "Oh, that is what love looks like," and created an internal relationship map.

However, if we saw our caregivers give each other the silent treatment and have explosive fights, we thought, "Oh, that is what love looks like," and once again created an internal relationship map.

> **Internal Maps:** The subconscious templates we create in childhood, which help us navigate how to exist in the world, based on what we experience and internalize, and then seek to repeat in adulthood.

We all have different internal maps because we have all had different experiences growing up. Our culture, geography, lineage, class, and of course parents, all play a part in our internal maps. Our maps are what we use, follow, and look to as we experience life. The problem with these internal maps is that we forget we are following them. We think that, if our relationships keep failing, it's our ex's fault, or if we keep getting fired, it's because all bosses suck.

Positive Bitch Tip: If you are not enjoying your current reality, it isn't because you're unlucky or were dealt a bad hand; rather, you are living according to an internal map that is aligned with your past instead of in alignment with your authentic frequency. If you're thinking, acting, or behaving in ways that are a means to an end, to get validation from others, connection, or love, you're living in accordance with an internal map that will not get you positive results long-term. You know you're plugged into your authentic self when you exist as you wish, not as you think you must be.

I witnessed partners fight using harsh language, but then be okay with each other an hour later. I thought that yelling at your partner was love, and that that was passion. When I got into an argument with my partner, I yelled. When he didn't return my sentiment, I was very confused. Subconsciously I was checking back to my relationship map, and according to that, if you love someone, you scream and fight.

I remember yelling, "You must not care about me! Where is your passion?"

When he didn't yell back, I thought, "Where is this on my map?"

My external reality, for the first time, was not aligning with my internal map. I didn't understand what I was experiencing. I saw love expressed in one way, and that one way was all I knew. Once we build a map, whether it's for relationships, anxiety, problem-solving, or anything else, this map becomes our foundation, which creates patterns. We give our power away when we blindly follow our internal maps, rather than our internal intuition. Our internal maps become our "truth," and we live within these routes.

Our "roots" become our routes. If we have a map for relationships, our ego is going to want to stick to that map, and that one route. Our ego knows its way around that map. It knows that route, the bumps in that route, and any possible threats along that route. Our ego clings to the routes it knows because it knows how to predict them. To our ego, predictability means safety. Even if our map only includes yelling and unhealthy behavior, our ego will favor this familiar route over a route that it has never experienced before, even if the new route is smoother. Our ego would rather live in an unhealthy relationship because it knows how to predict the fighting, and it does not know how to predict peace. Any route that is unpredictable to our ego will feel unsafe to us. This is why we get stuck in patterns of choosing partners who hurt us or are unhealthy for us. We do not keep going back to them because they are our one true love, they may just be familiar enough that they fit into our map. We know how to predict the fights, the emotional rollercoaster that follows, and the honeymoon stage that comes next. If we know it, we favor it.

It's hard to see life beyond our maps when we don't even realize we are living according to one. Many of us are unhappy with our reality because it is aligned with our internal map, rather than our authentic frequency. I aligned with a relationship, body, and overall reality that did not feel good to me because I was on autopilot, allowing my internal maps to run my life, rather than taking conscious control. About 95 percent of our day we are operating from our subconscious mind. When we allow the subconscious mind to drive our life, we are on autopilot.

Autopilot: Behaving and/or living unconsciously, according to our past maps, rather than using our conscious thinking mind.

When we are on autopilot, we are just going through the motions without even realizing what we are doing. By the time we are done going through the motions, we are often surprised we are done because we weren't present to begin with. When I was going through my breakup, I would wake up, get dressed for the gym, drive, and park. By the time I got to the gym, I didn't even remember driving there, because the whole time I was in my head. I wasn't being present; I was living on autopilot. Unless we start questioning our thoughts, feelings, and actions, we cannot go beyond living in our maps. If we continue to exist just by autopilot and we do not become conscious to ourselves, we will keep dragging our past maps into our present, instead of creating new maps that lead to new horizons.

Payouts

We give away our power when we repeatedly engage in actions that cause undesirable results, but yet never question them.

> **Positive Bitch Tip:** We don't do anything for shits and giggles. Whatever thought, action, or decision we make has some sort of payout, even if that payout is unknown to us consciously.

I kept procrastinating on my health journey because I was comfortable being overweight and known as the girl who had thyroid disease. My payout to procrastinating my healing was that I got to stay comfortable in my identity and I didn't have to try. Even though I didn't like the illness, my body, or being known as this identity, I didn't take actions to change it. Taking actions would force me to face that I was feeding my illness instead of trying to get better. I only knew how to be my body type. I didn't know what it would be like to release the weight, and I was afraid that if I tried, I would still fail. It wasn't healthy for me to remain the same, but because I had a subconscious fear of changing my identity, I kept choosing the same behaviors repeatedly. I didn't consciously know I was afraid to fail.

All I heard was, "I'll start my diet tomorrow," "I'm not that bad," or "This is just who I am, so there is nothing I can do."

These thoughts were just limiting beliefs. These beliefs were limiting my ability to heal. While I could hear these conscious thoughts, I didn't know that the subconscious payout was familiarity.

Dragging the Past into the Present

It can be confronting to realize that you're manifesting your daily life when every day looks the same, or when it's a reality you don't like. Our inner world corresponds to our outer one. If we feel chaotic, disorganized, and anxious internally, our outer world will form scenarios that match those feelings. This is known as the Law of Correspondence.

> **Law of Correspondence:** "As above, so below." All dimensions mirror and correspond to one another. What occurs in one dimension will affect the others. The most practical use of this law is to use it to understand that how we feel internally will manifest matching results externally.

Many people will try to change their outer reality first, when they really need to work on their inner one. I have been on and off diets since I was in elementary school. The diets would work temporarily, but eventually I would gain the weight back and end up where I originally started. This created an extremely annoying cycle of releasing and gaining weight for years. The problem was that I kept trying to focus on changing my outer reality: what I ate, what I restricted, and my workouts. Even when that worked temporarily, because I still saw myself as the same identity, had the same thoughts, and therefore had the same inner world, I would end up giving up on that diet and going backward.

> **Positive Bitch Tip:** Our inner world will always win because our programmed identity is stronger than our willpower. If you want to change your life, start by changing your inner world, because that is where your maps LIVE.

During my "break" with Mr. Gray Area, even though I had trouble sleeping, I desperately looked forward to it because it allowed some temporary relief from my reality.

Every morning I would remember the situation and think, "Ugh, that's right. I am CiiCii. I am broken-hearted, and I am lost."

Every morning I was plugging back into the same reality as the day before and therefore repeatedly manifesting further suffering. I would feel the same emotion as the day before, think the same thought, and focus on the same breakup. My days became so blurred together because I was dragging the same energetic signature into each day, aligning with similar circumstances each day. The crying didn't stop, the suffering didn't stop, the hurt didn't stop.

Our subconscious mind, being the receiver of information, doesn't know if something is happening in real time, or if we are just thinking about a past memory. My body was reexperiencing the trauma every day, thinking it was happening in real time. This is why breakups, or any traumatic experience, feel so intense even after the fact. If we think about a painful past experience, our subconscious mind thinks it's happening again. What does our body do? It continuously releases the same chemicals, such as cortisol and adrenaline, placing our body in the sympathetic nervous system, which causes burnout and exhaustion. My body thought every day that I was finding out again, and again, that Mr. Gray Area was being unfaithful because I kept thinking about the experience. I kept bringing my past into my present, which made it feel impossible to move on. He may have caused me pain, but I repeatedly tuned into the experience, causing myself to suffer.

82

To say I had no choice but to think and feel about this situation for days on end is simply a lie. To say I had no choice but to cry about this situation all day strips me of my free will. To say I had no choice but to revisualize painful memories daily is to say I am nothing more than a past memory. While waking up and immediately remembering the current circumstances of my life may have been out of my control, the second, third, fourth, and fifth thought were in my control, and I chose to think about things that were hurting me. Instead of focusing on a new beginning, or how I could expand my creativity, I harped on the one thing that I knew was going to make me miserable.

Recognizing Patterns

I noticed my attachment map most heavily activated in my adult intimate relationship. After Mr. Gray Area and I got back together—I'll now refer to him as Mr. Boyfriend—I started to notice a paralyzing fear every single time he left. I could not understand the emotions tied to the fear, nor the thoughts. I just knew I hated the feeling. My body was remembering something I consciously couldn't. I could feel the bodily sensations of my chest tightening, the emptiness in my stomach, and a longing for his presence, but I didn't understand why I felt this way. I rationally knew he had to go to work, and that he would be back the next week. I rationally knew he had to sometimes see his friends instead of me. I rationally knew it wasn't healthy for us to be on top of each other every single day, but none of these conscious thoughts could outweigh what my body was experiencing. Our body, like our mind, follows a map. If we lived mostly in survival mode, our body will keep following that map. Even if there is nothing to worry about, our body will enter into fight or flight mode simply out of trained habitual behavior.

As the weeks progressed, the paralyzing bodily sensations got more intense. I started to think back to when I had felt this feeling before, and just with that intention, memories started coming back to me. Every time Mr. Boyfriend would leave my house, my body would time-travel back to when my mom would threaten to leave the house. The exact same sick, paralyzed, empty feelings imprisoned my being. It became crystal clear: I feared abandonment, not only in the past with my mother, but in my present with my partner too.

About Our Attachment Map

It's common in the spiritual community to hear attachments are the worst thing to have, but I disagree. Our attachment system has been passed down from our ancestors as an advantage. Those who were attached to a tribe were more likely to survive than those who went out on their own. Survival of the fittest caused attachment systems to be passed down to us. Our attachment system isn't the problem; insecure attachments are. When we are insecurely attached to people, we will repeatedly think the same doomsday thoughts, feel the same anxieties, and attract the same dynamics.

Our attachment system is developed based on the caregiver we craved love from the most. Not only do we create an identity in response to this caregiver, but we often look for partners in our adult intimate relationships that will fit the dynamic we had with this caregiver. If you craved love from your father the most, but your father was often away on business trips, missed your soccer games, and couldn't connect to you emotionally, you most likely are drawn to potential partners who are "workaholics," are emotionally distant, or avoid intimacy altogether.

84

Why would we want the same dynamic we had as a child with the caregiver we craved love from the most? Even though our physical bodies age, our emotional bodies stay consistent with our child self, unless we are actively nourishing our wounds. I'm sure you have had the experience on your birthday when you turn one year older but you feel the same. Our physical bodies automatically age, while our emotional body does not mature unless we are consciously working to heal. Over time, we end up with a whole bunch of children walking around in adult bodies. Physically we see our loved ones, friends, and family age, but emotionally, most stay the same.

As an adult, that inner child who wanted love from that distant father still lives within us, and that inner child will seek to master that dynamic by trying to recreate the situation.

> **Inner Child:** Your younger self, especially the parts of you that felt unseen, unheard, or unloved, that lives within you energetically today. Your inner child is also your most playful side that comes out when you feel safe.

As a child we feel powerless in the adult world, but once we are an adult, our ego thinks we have more control over the dynamic; we can redo, and this time prove to ourselves that we are worthy of love.

My attachment map was already leaning toward an anxious attachment because I was constantly fearing my mom would abandon me. Then school made this attachment worse. One day in kindergarten, I was saving a seat for my friend. My teacher, for whatever reason, said I wasn't allowed to save a seat, screamed at me in front of everyone, and then made me sit at the all-boy table with a bunch of kids I'd never spoken to before. I was horrified. This only made the attachment to my mom worse. Before school, I would get ready, vomit, and then head onto the school bus. This became my normal routine. To make matters worse, one day after school, when the bus arrived at the end of my driveway earlier than usual for drop-off and my mom wasn't there, my bus driver wouldn't let me get off. It was a rule that a parent had to be at the end of the driveway or the bus driver could not let us leave. Even though an eighth-grade girl offered to walk me to my front door, the bus driver said no. The bus driver decided to leave, drop off everyone else, and then take me to a random parking lot. I don't remember how much time we spent in that parking lot, but it felt like hours. I was afraid because I didn't know what had happened to my mom, but also because I was alone with a random old man in a foreign parking lot and had no way of contacting anyone.

Finally, a call came through the speaker system on the bus—it was my school. They were able to contact the bus driver, and he dropped me off at home. While I was lucky enough to get back home, that still traumatized me. After this, I really didn't leave my mom's side, ever. Not even at friends' birthday parties did I want to detach from her. Cue the codependency. Not only did I never leave my mother's side, but if a sibling, or even my own father, was arguing with her, I stepped in to protect her. Whatever emotion she had, I absorbed it. Instead of me being CiiCii, I became just like another arm on my mother. I was an extension of her, rather than my own being. While we were extremely close, I was always waiting for the next moment when she might leave me. Our connection was close, yet felt inconsistent emotionally. Most days she would mother me, and some days it felt like I mothered her. When things felt good, I looked around for when they might go bad. I spent so much of my time worrying about my mom, her problems, and what she was feeling, I started to lose myself.

86

This created an anxiously codependent attachment map within my body. Even though my conscious mind wasn't thinking about these memories during my relationship with Mr. Boyfriend, my body remembered them. The experiences with Mr. Boyfriend leaving triggered my attachment system, which triggered my body into a dumpster fire of SOS signals. I was reliving the fear of being abandoned by my mother, now with my boyfriend. This nightmare of a pattern continued into my adult relationship because I never healed that inner child wound. What we do not heal will continue in the form of lessons throughout life. Lessons will continue until we change our internal map, think differently, feel differently, and therefore act differently. If we show up differently, our reality cannot show up the same way.

How to Take Your Power Back from Patterns

❤ *When you are going about your day, I invite you to start questioning which reality you are aligning with by asking yourself, "Is this in alignment with who I am, or who I was?"*

Taking pauses throughout your day prevents you from running solely on autopilot. Asking yourself this question before making decisions allows you to practice mindfulness so that you may live in a way that feels good. Pausing to consciously respond, rather than subconsciously react, allows us to look through the conscious window of our present and decide in the now. Our connection to our authentic self lives in the present moment. If you want to act like your authentic self, you must connect to your authentic self. This requires grounding yourself in the present moment.

Living miserably—while it unfortunately has become normalized because so many people have fallen prey to their ego—is not how we are meant to live. While we came to earth to learn, we did not come here to be miserable. Yes, we will experience a range of human emotions. We will be faced with lower-vibrational emotions, but this should not be our home-base emotion. Negative emotions are a second or third base. They are bases we will slide through, experience for a moment, but will ultimately leave behind. Where we spend most of our time, our home base, should be a high-vibrational base. One in which we enjoy life, enjoy our hobbies, enjoy the people around us. If we are not enjoying our reality, it isn't because we are bad or deserve to be punished; it is because we are aligning with our map more than our authentic frequency.

To step out of our map, we must step out of our subconscious mind by being mindful with our decisions. Checking in with ourselves throughout our day creates space for us to live consciously, as a daily participant in our life, rather than being a slave to our past.

Our Focus Determines Our Feel

Last time I checked, you weren't a puppet to be played with—you were a Positive Bitch, and Positive Bitches take responsibility for their focus. Where focus goes, energy follows. If I were to keep replaying the memory of my breakup, putting my focus on a past pain, my energy would follow and drop into a low vibe. What we pay attention to will affect how we feel. There is no point in repeatedly revisiting memories that don't serve you.

> **Positive Bitch Tip:** Your happiness depends on you. If you are not happy, it is a YOU problem. If you want to feel happy, you must stop thinking about things that make you feel upset.

Many people are emotionally addicted to feeling self-pity, anxiety, or even like a victim. If someone is in a bad mood once or twice, you know they're just having a bad day. If someone is in a bad mood every day, you assume that's just who they are. The more we practice an emotion, the better we get at it. While we are not our emotions, if we practice an emotion enough times, we end up embodying the emotion rather than our authentic self. What was once an emotion becomes the cornerstone of our personality, and what others will know us for.

♥ *If you keep going back to a low-vibe thought which is creating a low-vibe emotion, interrupt this pattern by asking, "What am I getting from this emotion?" and/or "What is this emotion trying to teach me?"*

We know everything we do, think, and/or feel has some sort of payout. If the payout is being comfortable, how can you create safety for yourself in a way that can serve you? Some ways to create safety are watching a show you've seen before to provide comfort, listening to peaceful music, loving your pet, or spending time in nature. Once you understand why you keep going back to the same pattern, you can create new ways to healthily receive what you need.

Interrupting Patterns

How can you interrupt those intense feelings that seem to just happen? We must peer into the patterns we are presented with. I don't believe a pattern would keep showing up if it had nothing to teach us. The pattern is pointing you toward a greater truth, emotion, or wound, that needs your love and attention. When you feel an intense fear or emotion, you want to pause and ground yourself. Instead of disassociating, going out, drinking, or eating, you want to look straight at this feeling.

First, create space for the emotion to have the spotlight. Try identifying where you are feeling this emotion and what it feels like.

For example, "I feel an emptiness in my stomach, and I feel afraid to be alone."

Secondly, feel the emotion. If you need to cry, cry. If you need to scream into a pillow, scream into a pillow. If that isn't feeling good, try punching a pillow. I personally like to put on City Girls and shake my ass till the sun comes up, but hey, maybe that's just me. Any sort of movement is welcomed during the release phase. If you have ever seen two dogs playing, when they step away from each other, you may have noticed they will both wiggle their bodies. Dogs instinctively know that after an interaction, they must wiggle their bodies to release the energy from the prior interaction, rather than holding onto it. Movement helps us release energy, so girl, if you need to twerk, do the damn thing.

> **Say to yourself, "I allow myself to release all that no longer serves me," and pay attention to how your body begins to feel lighter.**

Thirdly, ground yourself in your body. Look around the room: what do you see? What day is it? What are you currently doing? Bring yourself back to your own experience in your own body. What is your body doing? Where are your feet? Your hands? Wrap your arms around yourself, feel your own body, and anchor down.

Fourthly, I invite you to give your inner child what she is craving. If your inner child is craving connection and feels abandoned, how can you connect to her? You can do something you used to love to do as a child, color, go for a walk, or even meditate. If your inner child needs some time to disconnect from others, how can you give her that? Maybe refocusing on a current project or doing a face mask can allow her to feel relaxed. We want to essentially create safety for our inner child to feel okay so we can nurse the wound that created the pattern, rather than re-create the pattern itself.

What We Don't Heal, We Repeat

Keep in mind, this is not about blaming anyone.

> **Positive Bitch Tip:** Positive Bitches are victors. We cannot
> be victors if we are simultaneously claiming to be victims.
> Our parents tried their best with what they knew. This
> isn't about blaming your past, but proactively healing
> your now. We are not going to point our finger, but rather
> acknowledge our past just as it was. No better and no worse.
> The past is over, and all you have now is you, your present
> moment, and what you do with it.

To heal your attachment map, you must make a connection with your
inner child. Most of our inner child is stored in our subconscious. I
had no idea I'd recreated the dynamic I had with my mother with my
boyfriend, and I had no clue I was codependent because it was all I've
ever known.

What signaled to me that something was off was the underlying
feeling of abandonment anytime he left. When we feel something
that isn't pleasant, that feeling is trying to communicate with us.
This feeling was trying to tell me that I had a wound that was wide
open. We cannot put a Band-Aid on a bullet hole. We often try to
escape these uncomfortable feelings when these feelings are trying
to teach us. This feeling of abandonment wasn't a red flag about
the behavior of my boyfriend, but rather a green light for me to
discover myself.

I knew rationally that Mr. Boyfriend wasn't doing anything that
should warrant such an intense response, so I turned inward. If you
feel pulled to the "f-boys" or keep aligning with someone who is hot

91

and cold, this is related to your attachment map, and the pattern will not shift until you shift. It's not that you like mean men, or that you aren't lovable; it is that you have learned one way to attach in love, and it is not in alignment with your core frequency and so does not feel good. You can relearn how to love and how to attach, but first we must unlearn what was originally programmed.

Some of us deeply fear being left, some of us deeply fear getting too close, and some of us have a whole bunch of fears intertwined into our being. What matters is learning to regulate your inner child so that you may exist within relationships in the present, rather than recreating those of your past.

Use these prompts to make connection to your inner child, and shed light on your attachment map.

(*What was the dynamic I had with the parent I craved love from the most?*

(*How was my last partner(s) or current partner like the parent I craved love from?*

(*How does my last or current relationship mirror the dynamic I had as a child?*

(*What unpleasant feelings does this attachment evoke?*

(*How was this same unpleasant feeling brought out as a child?*

(*What does my inner child want to feel, see, hear, and experience?*

(*How can I give my inner child what she is craving?*

4

Positive Bitches Use Their Emotions, They Aren't Used by Them

Taking Your Power Back from Your Emotions

Conscious Question:

"What Is This Emotion Telling Me?"

The Emotion Hiding Under Your Bed

The lingo around lower-vibrational emotions is weird AF. When someone shows emotions, common responses include:

"Don't cry."
"Stop being so sensitive."
"Suck it up."
"Let's go out and forget about it."
"There are people who have it worse."

We have been taught to escape, ignore, and push down our emotions when our emotions never meant any harm in the first place. We especially try to get away from emotions that feel "dark" or "icky" because they aren't always enjoyable in the moment. We aren't realizing that, by avoiding our feelings, we are avoiding our healing. We must reframe how we interact with our emotions if we want to use them instead of them using us.

Positive Bitch Tip: Emotions are messengers, not monsters. If we try to run from our emotions, our emotions will forever haunt us. Running from our emotions keeps us stuck, as they will keep drawing us toward similar situations, leading to the same emotional outcomes. These situations may feature different people, places, or details, but ultimately, they will lead us back to the same emotional wound we have been trying to escape since we were a child. This is how our emotions can haunt us.

I had to learn the hard way that being in denial of an emotion does not get rid of it; rather, it prolongs the experience of that emotion.

Don't Be Afraid of the Dark

We cannot outrun our own darkness, and we are not meant to. Darkness is where growth begins. Seeds germinate in dark dirt, babies develop in the darkness of a womb, and, at the end of every dark tunnel, one can find the light. Instead of running from emotions that feel "dark," I invite you to dance with this darkness. In facing these darker emotions, you can bring them to the light and transmute the dark energy into empowering light energy.

E-Motions

Emotions, like everything else in this quantum world, are energy. The word *emotion* stems from a Latin term "emovere," which means to move out. Emotions' natural state is movement. We can break down the word emotion as e-motion or energy in motion to have a deeper understanding of what emotions actually are. Our emotions are meant to move out of us, not live within us forever. When we try to push down an emotion, we create secondary problems. Not allowing ourselves to feel will trap the energy in our bodies, which can cause autoimmune disease, acne, weight gain, and other side effects. We know that energy cannot be created or destroyed, but it can be transformed. I like to think about energy like water. Water can transform into different states: vapor, liquid, and solid. E-motions can play a similar role. What does this look like? I thought you would never ask!

1. **Water Vapor:** I used to subconsciously think, "I am not enough," which caused me to feel empty.

Energy can enter the body in the form of a thought. This thought form may or may not be conscious. I wasn't aware of this thought, but it caused me to feel hollow. Whether a thought is conscious or not, thoughts can cause a biochemical reaction in the body which then causes an emotion. Emotions are largely influenced by thoughts, but not every thought causes an immediate emotional reaction or an emotional reaction at all. Thoughts are powerful because they create mind movies, and mind movies are very good at convincing our subconscious mind that what we see in our mind is indeed fact.

While I wasn't aware of this thought, I was aware of a slight emptiness I would feel here and there. It was elusive and fleeting, but it was a feeling that always lingered in the background. At this point, this emotion was like water vapor because it was barely there. I didn't know why I was feeling the emptiness, and I wasn't aware that it even was emptiness. I just thought I would feel "off" sometimes. The emotion was not tangible, but rather misty, like vapor.

2. **Liquid:** Eventually, I practiced this subconscious thought and emotion enough times that it began to get louder by manifesting into my reality.

We know that our dominant thoughts and emotions become our energetic signature or "magnet" from which we manifest experiences. I repeatedly manifested experiences where I felt like I was not enough. I perceived this in friendships, relationships, and even in my work. I was always striving for perfection because I thought that what I had to offer was not good enough.

My emotion that was once vapor began to liquify and become more real. My manifested experiences reaffirmed my subconscious thought and fleeting feeling of not being good enough and brought me to tears countless times. The emotion of not feeling good enough began to become tangible. I could feel this emotion releasing from my body through my tears, and I would feel my throat tense up.

The good news is, if you allow yourself to feel your emotions, you are allowing the energy to be released. This may look like crying, talking to a professional, or even working out and sweating. The bad news is, most of the time we push down our emotions, and try to escape them by a maladaptive coping mechanism, like drinking, binge eating, gambling, or overspending. This traps the energy within our bodies. This doesn't allow the energy to be in motion, which causes greater harm. Trying to avoid our emotions turns an initial problem of escapism into a secondary problem of possible addiction and other *dis-ease* in the body. Disease is literally our body not at ease. Holding onto our emotions stunts our organs' functions, which causes our body to dysregulate. This can look like digestive issues, pain in the body, weight gain, or autoimmune disease. Our body can't operate optimally when we are constantly thinking of a perceived threat. Our body will assume all our attention needs to be on the perceived threat, rather than regulating its systems. Secondary problems have long-term side effects. While maladaptive coping mechanisms numb us, giving up a moment of temporary relief, they deprive us in the long run.

3. **Ice:** The energy of "not feeling good enough" solidified into acne and weight gain.

While I did shed tears over experiences where I felt rejected, I didn't know those tears were stemming from the subconscious thought of not feeling good enough. I felt sad but couldn't identify why. Whenever this feeling was triggered, I began to binge-eat.

I used to say, "Ugh, I don't even know what just happened, I blacked out."

I would look down and a whole sleeve of Oreos would mysteriously be missing. Could I be the drama? I would eat so fast that I wasn't even conscious of what exactly I was eating. I was trying to disassociate from the pain as fast as possible, and my way to do that was bingeing. I didn't know what I was feeling, I didn't know why I was upset, and I didn't know how to stop it. I did know how to eat, so that is what I did. I felt like I was not good enough, and through the maladaptive behavior of binge eating, I literally became more by gaining weight.

> **Positive Bitch Tip:** When we feel we are not enough or we feel we are not worthy, we will overcompensate somewhere else to become more. Whether we try to become more by subconsciously gaining weight or buying more material goods, we will find a way to fill any holes we perceive in ourselves.

For me, I didn't feel like I had any control, I felt small in this world, and gaining weight literally made me bigger. What started out as a fleeting thought became more real through emotion and solidified through weight gain.

Emotions Are a Life Sentence, Not a Death Sentence

Our emotions are meant to be used as a compass to navigate our time here on earth; they are not meant to hurt us. Only a fragment of our soul can exist within our bodies. Our higher self, which is our connection to God, is another part of a soul that exists beyond our body. Our higher self "downloads" emotions into our bodies to help us understand our experiences on earth. Feeling a high-vibrational emotion, like happiness, freedom, or love, is a sign that what you are experiencing is in vibrational alignment with your energetic signature. Feeling a low-vibrational emotion, like fear, grief, or anger, is a sign that what you are experiencing is not in vibrational alignment with your energetic signature.

High-vibration: Positive qualities, practices, feelings, thoughts, places, people, and circumstances. When in alignment with something that is high in vibration, associated feelings may include happiness, freedom, love, joy, expansiveness, and creativity.

Low-vibration: Negative qualities, practices, feelings, thoughts, places, people, and circumstances. When in alignment with something that is low in vibration, associated feelings may include powerlessness, grief, depression, anxiety, and anger.

When I was in college, what felt "good" to me was working out, drinking celery juice, and making music. As you may know, that isn't in line with the typical college experience. Even though most people around me preferred going out to my celery juice, partying every weekend didn't feel good to me. Working out with green juices was in vibrational alignment with me, which is why it felt good. Partying every weekend was not in vibrational alignment with me, which is why it felt bad. Things that feel good to us and are good for us are green lights to move toward. Things that do not feel good to us, and aren't good for us, are red lights. When we hit a red light, we need to pause and figure out where to redirect ourselves. We wouldn't know what we like and what we don't like without our emotions guiding us. Our emotions help us know what we should pursue, what we should move away from, and how to move forward in the world. If we listen to our emotions, they will lead us to our dream partner, career, and purpose.

There is no one-size-fits-all when it comes to high vibrations. What is high-vibe for one person could be low-vibe for another. What is high in vibration for one person may differ for another, so don't compare your lifestyle with someone else's. Focus on what feels good to you, not what others are doing. When you are focused on you, it's easier to have awareness of when low-vibe emotions are present.

> **Positive Bitch Tip:** Low-vibe emotions are not negative; they are information about our environment. Many people try to avoid low-vibe emotions because they think they're "bad," but they, like high-vibe emotions, are just data.

Ignoring our emotions would be like ignoring a fire alarm. The purpose of a fire alarm is the same as our emotions: to alert us to our surroundings. Fire alarms and emotions alike should be listened to, not ignored. Sometimes fire alarms go off by mistake, but we still respond with caution when we hear one. We do not have to stop, drop and roll the minute a fire alarm goes off; we do not need to become hysterical; all we must do is listen and act accordingly. We want to do the same thing with our emotions.

100

Our emotions aren't "must dos"; rather, they are "listen tos." If we take action the second we feel an emotion, we are going to most likely regret that action. When I got into an argument with Mr. Boyfriend, I would do my usual thing, which was to verbally explode. I would use harsh language, and then later feel terrible and anxious that he would leave me. I've learned over time that feeling low-vibrational during a conversation with him is not an excuse to explode, it's an invitation to hear my higher self. Exploding my anger onto him wasn't a "must do"; it was meant to be a "listen to" why I was so upset. I cannot understand myself if I don't create space in which I can hear myself. I then created something called "Yellow Light," which is a conversation break technique.

Instead of blowing up, I'll tell him, "Yellow Light," which means, "Slow down, I need some time to process my emotions."

> **Yellow Light:** Technique to be used when you need time to process your inner emotional world. When in a heated argument, or feeling unsure of how to respond, say, either in your head or aloud, "Yellow Light," and take a pause to regulate yourself. In this time, you can wash your face, go for a walk, or journal to understand what you're feeling.

I'll say this anytime the conversation is getting heated and I need to take a break to understand what I'm feeling. He knows I am not giving him the silent treatment or trying to disrespect him, but I do need time to hear myself to allow our conversation to be helpful rather than harmful. Exploding from your emotions isn't fun for you, and I'll tell you now, it sucks for the other person too. If you cannot handle your inner emotional storm, neither can the person sitting across from you. We have to exist within our own body for the rest of our lives; taking time to learn how to regulate ourself is worth it for us, and our current or future partner.

When you take responsibility and hear out your emotions, you can learn to regulate yourself, which allows for deeper authentic connection with yourself and others. They won't have to walk on eggshells, they will be able to be authentic with you, and you'll feel so much more at ease. When I say, "Yellow Light," I will then pause and take a shower, go for a walk, or even read. After having some space, I can come back to the conversation with clarity rather than emotional overload. You will find that your emotions oxidize like makeup. You know what I mean—like when you first put your foundation on and it matches perfectly, but then two hours later, it's completely orange and two shades darker than your skin tone.

101

Yeah, emotions do that too. Emotions change over time because they are in motion. An emotion may feel very heavy at first, but if you give it some time to move around, you will be able to have greater clarity about what you truly value, rather than what you temporarily feel. Instead of continuously being stuck in a cycle of blow up, feel bad, be afraid he'll leave, apologize, blow up, feel bad, be afraid he'll leave, apologize, and so on, I can now just say, "Yellow Light." When you become curious about your emotions, instead of furious that they're there, you allow yourself to hear your higher self, constructive conversation can happen, and you'll live a life that leads to greater healing.

Pain Can Be the Portal If You Let It

Pain can lead us back home to ourselves. When I was dealing with my anxious attachment map in relation to my boyfriend, feeling abandoned all the time, this caused me great pain. If this pain had never been triggered, I would not have known there was something that needed to be healed within me. Our pain can be transmuted into our power when we take responsibility for our e-motions and get curious about the root of them. This pain showed me what wounds were exposed so that I could nourish them with love. Instead of acting out from my attachment map, I had the chance to find myself and go back home to my home frequency of Positive Bitch Energy.

Taking Your Power Back from Your Emotions

Since we have been programmed to push down our emotions, many of us feel that we aren't allowed to feel anything. To take our power back, we must give ourselves permission to let our emotions come to the surface so that the energy can be transmuted into Positive Bitch Frequency.

> To give yourself permission, say, "I, (state your name), have the divine right to feel my emotions completely, fully, and thoroughly. I give myself permission to acknowledge and experience the energy in motion that is within me. I welcome my emotions to the forefront of my being. I am feeling to heal, and it feels good to do so."

Triggers, Temper Tantrums, and Toddlers

I know what you're thinking, "CiiCii, I'm just going to live a life where I avoid all my triggers, and then I'll be happy."

Yeah, I've heard that one before. Spoiler alert: trying to avoid everything that triggers you is avoiding the human experience; it's also just annoying. Part of existing as a human is feeling a wide range of human emotions. There is nothing wrong with experiencing a low-vibe emotion, as it's acting as a compass to this reality. It's communicating to you that something is not in alignment with your vibration. If you need to feel a low-vibe emotion, just feel the low-vibe emotion and attempt to understand what it's trying to tell you.

Ask the emotion, "What are you trying to convey to me?"

Feeling a low vibration may make you feel bad; you do not need to make yourself feel worse by hating yourself for experiencing the emotion. Hating yourself for feeling an e-motion will not lead you to healing, but to more hurt.

104

When we are triggered, a wound isn't being created; rather, that trigger is poking at a wound that is already within us. Ever see an adult act out, start screaming, crying, and acting like a toddler? Maybe you even saw that adult in the mirror...it's okay, we've all been there. Adult temper tantrums are a sign that an emotion has been locked away for a very long time. Triggers hurt because they're like putting a knife in a wound that already exists. Deep wounds do not heal themselves; they require us to nurture them with love. If we have many triggers, it's because we have pushed down many emotions and didn't allow them to be released in the moment. What's really hurting when we are triggered isn't our present self, but our inner child who's been trying to push everything down for years on end. It makes sense that when we are triggered, our actions revert back to a three-year-old, because it's the inner three-year-old that is hurting.

Positive Bitch Tip: Triggers aren't tragic; they offer new life. Every time we are triggered, it's an invitation to reparent our inner child with love. It's a chance to apply spiritual and emotional Neosporin to that wound that has been open for so long. It's an opportunity for you to validate yourself and your emotions. Facing triggers requires a mindset shift. Instead of seeing moments of being triggered as negative, and wanting to run from them, see it as an opportunity to transmute negative energy. If we have held onto negative energy for a long time, it isn't going to feel so good coming up; this is why we try to avoid the low-vibe emotions. It may lead us to cry or feel anxious, but that's a side effect of releasing it. It's like milk. If we keep milk for too long, it will spoil. If we try to keep our emotions in for too long, they will spoil too. The longer we keep milk in the fridge, the smellier, clumpier, and grosser it's going to get. The more we try to push down our e-motions, especially lower-vibe e-motions, the smellier, clumpier, and more painful it will be when we release it.

105

How to Feel Your Emotions

When toddlers release their e-motions, they do it right. Toddlers are very present and express emotion whenever they feel it, unless they are told they cannot. When they're upset, they cry without inner judgment, releasing the e-motion, and then five minutes later they're fine again. We on the other hand get upset with our boss in the morning and carry this on our back until we can black out on the weekend. I'm not telling you to cry during a board meeting, but I am saying to acknowledge when something doesn't feel good and take a minute afterwards to be present with that emotion. When you feel upset, take a "Yellow Light" and pause to feel your emotion. Instead of reacting to a negative emotion and calling your boss a name, or having to black out on Friday night, learn to respond to your emotions by creating space for them to be seen, heard, and loved. Don't judge them, criticize them, or fight them; just observe them, and lovingly reparent yourself with kind words back to feeling okay again.

I literally hug myself in moments where I am feeling deeply upset or alone. I know this sounds weird, but it feels magical. Our own touch is super powerful. Just hugging ourselves can lower cortisol, the stress hormone, in our body and lead us back to a rest and digest state.

While hugging myself, I will ask, "What does my inner child need to hear, feel, or see right now to help her feel safe?"

Let's say my inner child needs to be validated because she's always heard, "You're just sensitive." Instead of ignoring my emotions like other adults may have in the past, I will validate my inner child by acknowledging the emotion coming up and allowing it to be expressed. If this means crying, I will cry. If this means I need to journal about what I'm feeling, I will journal. I'll do what I feel I should do, but the one thing I will not do is ignore that there are e-motions running through my body that want to be released.

I recommend carving time out of your schedule to feel whatever it is you need to feel. Trying to push down our emotions will lead to secondary problems, but feeling so emotional we can't get anything done *EVER* is not helpful either. We need to feel our emotions, but we also don't want them running our lives. We need boundaries even with our emotions. Set a timer for twenty-five to forty-five minutes and let your emotions run wild. We are setting a timer because realistically we can only actively feel an emotion for so long. Eventually that emotion leaves our body, but we retrigger more low-vibrational emotions by habitually thinking another low-vibrational thought. Instead of going through a self-induced trigger cycle, we want to just release the e-motion. If we don't interrupt the cycle, it will look like this:

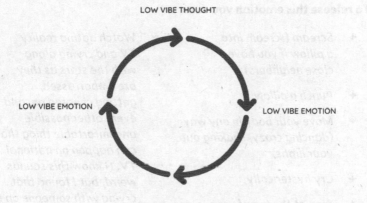

LOW VIBE THOUGHT

LOW VIBE EMOTION

LOW VIBE EMOTION

LOW VIBE THOUGHT

When we release the e-motion instead of retriggering ourselves through another low-vibe thought, we break out of this habitual emotional prison and take our power back. No one can keep Positive Bitches captive, not even our own emotions. These processing sessions are like an emotional recess for your inner child. You can schedule them daily or weekly, it's up to you. You can spend your emotional recess in several different ways, but the first thing you'll want to do is just name the emotion you are going to be hanging out with.

Ask yourself:

- ♥ *What is the emotion I am experiencing?*
- ♥ *Where is it in my body?*
- ♥ *What does this emotion feel like in my body?*

If you aren't sure of the emotion you are feeling, it's okay. Just having awareness that there is energy coursing through your body is enough to know it must be released. Now, it's the fun part.

To release this emotion you can:

- ✦ *Scream (scream into a pillow if you have close neighbors)*
- ✦ *Punch a pillow*
- ✦ *Move your body in any way (dancing crazy, shaking out your limbs)*
- ✦ *Cry hysterically*
- ✦ *Sing at the top of your lungs to the saddest or angriest of songs*
- ✦ *Burn palo santo or white sage to absorb/cleanse the low vibrations*

- ✦ *Watch dating reality TV and crying along with the stars as they are embarrassed, getting cheated on, and every other possible uncomfortable thing that can happen on national TV. (I know this sounds weird, but I found that crying with someone on the TV allowed me to locate my emotions and release them. It didn't matter that I was identifying with the star on the screen, what mattered is that I released the energy.)*

While these options work well, I personally like to channel my e-motions into different activities. At the end of the day, e-motions are just energy. We can use our upset or anger and channel it into many different forms that will not only release the energy, but shift our mood too.

This includes but is not limited to:

+ Creating a social media post
+ Playing an instrument
+ Singing (any song)
+ Painting/drawing
+ Dancing
+ Writing/journaling
+ Inner child activity (any creative activity you enjoyed as a child)

+ Making a vision board
+ Working out/yoga
+ Nature walk
+ Meditation/breath work
+ Cooking
+ Signing up for a new class (ex. pottery, yoga, dance)
+ Prayer

When we are participating in any of these activities, we are using that low-vibe energy and releasing it through either our creativity or movement. Once we release this stagnant emotion, our energy naturally lifts, and we feel better. We have taken that low-vibrational energy and transmuted it through our action into high-vibrational energy. The energy that once weighed us down is now converted into energy that empowers us.

> **Positive Bitch Tip:** Feeling a negative emotion, or channeling a negative emotion, isn't a negative experience but a positive opportunity to shift your energy to create yourself rather than destroy yourself.

My point is, energy is energy at the end of the day, so if it's there, use it to your advantage.

Highly Sensitives

Now it's time to shout out my Positive Bitches who feel everything. If you're like me, you have been told your whole life you are too sensitive. Sensitivity is a superpower when you use it to pick up on others' energy and have compassion for others. However, too much of anything isn't great. If we have no boundaries with our emotions or with others' e-motions, we may become a slave to others' energy or to external circumstance, and lose sight of ourselves. This is self-abandonment. Instead of trying to control other people and situations, take control of your inner world. This allows you to not have to avoid your reality, but rather shift it to your liking.

When in Doubt, Look at Your Values

If your emotions are all over the place, which, hey it happens, try acting in alignment with your values rather than your emotions. Emotions change much more than our values do. If we follow our values, rather than act out from our emotions, we can remain in a vibration that feels good to us. I know I highly value my health. If I feel upset, instead of drowning in my sadness, I will still move toward my value of health, and I will do a light workout. I'll listen to my emotion and take things slow, but I won't let it dictate my life and take away from what I value. By remaining loyal to my values even when I don't *feel* like it, I can shift my energy into a higher-vibrational state.

Positive Bitch Activation

This is important to understand, especially for manifestation. We cannot change our future circumstances by using the same energy that created our current circumstances.

) **Positive Bitch Tip:** Circumstances shift when we shift our
(focus, which shifts our energy.

If you want to manifest money, a relationship, or a new home, focusing on your current circumstance—how you do not have money, a relationship, or a new home—will only keep you manifesting the same circumstance. Every single subject—money, relationships, homes, etc.—has a lack frequency and an abundance frequency. Thinking about the lack of what you want will manifest more lack.

To manifest a new circumstance, you must create new energy. To create new energy, you must have a new focus or intention, which will create new emotion. As I've mentioned previously, we cannot simultaneously be a victim and a victor. This is because feeling like a victim is on a completely different frequency than feeling like a victor. Someone who is manifesting from a victim point of attraction has a completely different focus and emotion than someone who is manifesting from a victor point of attraction. We cannot manifest circumstances that make us feel like a victor if we are creating from a victim point of attraction.

If you want to manifest Positive Bitch circumstances, you must manifest FROM a Positive Bitch point of attraction, meaning your focus and e-motion must be in alignment with Positive Bitch Frequency.

Focus that is aligned with PBF looks like:

+ *Positive Thoughts*

+ *Having faith that all is unfolding for you*

+ *Envisioning your life exactly as you wish it to be*

+ *Focusing on solutions rather than the problem*

+ *Interrupting negative non-serving thoughts*

Emotions that are aligned with PBF feel like:

+ *Freedom*

+ *Joy*

+ *Expansion*

+ *Healing*

+ *Excitement*

+ *Nourishment*

+ *Abundance*

+ *Love*

❤ ***Start asking yourself, "Where am I manifesting from? Am I manifesting from a Positive Bitch point of attraction or a Negative Bitch point of attraction?"***

Negative Bitch Point of Attraction looks and feels like lack and fear.

112

If you are acting, focusing, and feeling from a Positive Bitch point of attraction, you are good to go. If you are acting, focusing, and feeling from fear, or any other low-vibe emotion, stop and readjust.

Thank yourself for having awareness and releasing that e-motion to the light:

> **"I'm proud of myself for having awareness that I am experiencing something that isn't in alignment. I thank this emotion for serving me, and I release it to the light."**

Positive Bitch Tip: To readjust your energy, say, "Positive Bitchitude Activate, Activate, Activate," three times aloud while clapping your hands. Using this mantra while clapping your hands will shake up your energy and allow you to act from a new standpoint, a higher-vibrational standpoint to be exact.

Remember, you must shift internally before you can shift externally.

Once you interrupt the lower-vibe point of attraction with the mantra, refocus on what makes you feel good. You can apply either self-care or soul-care activities. Self-care activities include face masks, booking a massage, watching a rom-com, or even making some tea and reading. Soul care involves going deeper by journaling, getting into nature, and connecting to your inner child to raise your vibration. One of my favorite ways to get myself into a PBF is to listen to motivational movie music and envision my dream life. Trust me, it's way more fun to focus on how everything can go right rather than how everything can go wrong. As I focus on my desires unfolding, my whole body tingles with excitement, and just like that, my point of attraction has shifted.

The more you practice tapping into Positive Bitch Frequency, the better you will get at it. If Positive Bitch Frequency was at one time foreign, it will start to feel natural as you are building a habit out of connecting to this high-vibe energy. Once in PBF, enjoy how good it feels. When you feel you have shifted to a higher vibration, show gratitude and celebrate what you've done.

> **"I'm thankful for my ability to shift my own energy. I love taking responsibility for my own life. It feels good to be a conscious creator."**

One of my favorite ways to stay in PBF is to remind myself, regardless of what is happening in my external reality, that everything is happening "*for* me, not *to* me." Instead of being emotionally reactive to my external environment, I remind myself, no matter what is going on, it is happening FOR me, so I do not need to worry. Instead of being jerked around by people or places, I take responsibility for my focus, which nurtures my emotion, and allows me to anchor into Positive Bitch Frequency.

114

5

Positive Bitches Rest on Their Pedestals and Attract, They Do Not Chase

Taking Your Power Back from People

Conscious Question: "WWAPBD— What Would a Positive Bitch Do?"

Friends, F-Boys, and Foes, Oh My

We align with many different characters along our journey here on earth. The question I found myself constantly asking was, why *this* person, but not *that* person? It comes down to our vibration. We attract the vibration we emit. I know what you're thinking.

"CiiCii, you lost me. I did not attract this f-boy who is ruining my life."

Unfortunately, not all our attracting is conscious or purposeful. If we are operating about 95 percent of our day from our subconscious mind, that means we are mostly attracting from an unknown point of attraction. We have to become conscious to ourselves, not just who we think we are, but *all* of who we are, to attract better connections into our life.

Different Types of People We Attract

Those of Like Vibration: The Law of Attraction states that like attracts like. Similar particles will always move toward each other. At our smallest atomic level, we are vibrating particles, a.k.a. energy. This means you will be drawn to like-vibrational people and activities. If you like yoga, you will be drawn to yoga classes where you will meet other yogis.

Those of Opposite Vibration: We attract what we really want and what we really *don't* want. If I have an extreme hatred for rude people, I will attract rude people. Whatever traits we push down in ourselves becomes part of our "shadow self."

> **Shadow Self:** The parts of ourselves we deem "unacceptable" or "unlovable" and try to hide. Although we do not allow ourselves to express these traits, it does not mean we don't have the capability to embody them.

Being in denial of a trait does not mean it is not part of you; it simply means you are denying that it's there. The more I push down the part of myself that can be rude, the more I will hate rudeness in others, and the more I will attract it into my experience. We must make amends with all of ourself. As humans, we all can be loud but also quiet, rude but also kind, and so on. We can experience and express a whole spectrum of characteristics. The more you allow yourself room to experience all different traits, the less you will hate them in others. We will discuss how to bring your shadow into the light in further detail later in this chapter.

Those You Have Beliefs About: Our mind will magnify whatever we think about. This is in part due to our reticular activating system in our brainstem (RAS).

> **Reticular Activating System:** Acts as a filtration center based on our own beliefs so we can process the external world.

If we were to try to take in all the information we see every day, our bodies would be in overdrive. We have the RAS to help us filter information in the external world so we can process the world around us. The caveat to this is that the RAS filters information based on our own biases. If I think all bosses suck, my RAS will constantly be scanning to see when my boss will do something that may irritate me. My boss may not actually suck, but because I already have this assumption, I am more likely to pick up on when they do something wrong and magnify it. On top of this, my belief that "all bosses suck" will attract bosses that are less likely to be good. If you keep attracting a type of person you do not like, ask yourself, "Do I have a belief about people like this that is causing me to repeatedly attract them into my life?"

Those That Fit Into Our Story: This category is most seen in our intimate relationships. If I grew up with an alcoholic mother, absent father, and two little siblings, I may have stepped up into the role of the caregiver to get connection from my mother. As we move through our lives, we forget that we create roles to be seen, heard, and loved. If I needed to be a caregiver as a child, I most likely will align with someone who also needs me to be their caregiver as an adult. This potential partner may be an alcoholic themselves, constantly ill, a hypochondriac, helpless, or generally chaotic. Either way, this partner will reconfirm my narrative that I am in fact a caregiver. We will align with others who reconfirm who we think we are.

Positive Bitch Tip: I frequently hear my clients tell me they feel like they're addicted to their ex. They aren't actually addicted to their ex-dude, but rather to the *dynamic* they had with that dude. We are addicted to reconfirming our old faulty roles instead of deciding who we wish to be in the present. If someone who is fulfilling a role in our life leaves, not only does it hit upon the hurt from our original caregiver, but the wound becomes deeper as this person hurts us in the present. This is why love can hurt like hell. We are hurting both presently and in our past, as an adult and a child, simultaneously.

Those Aligned with Our Subconscious Junk/Unknown Energy Forms: I want to make it clear that it is not our fault when we align with someone who is in a very low vibration...like very low. If someone has seriously hurt you, that is **NOT** your fault. If you were a victim of physical or verbal abuse, this is not your fault; it never has been and never will be. You may have been victimized, but you are more than a victim. You can and will overcome whatever you have experienced. As humans, we have a lot of energy that can attach onto us without us even knowing. You were born an innocent child and did not ask for abuse; however, we can pick up negative energy from a place, another person, or even negative thoughts. That is how we can align with horrible circumstances. We do not mean to pick up this negative energy, but it can happen. If someone has tricked you into giving your power away in the past, that has nothing on you now. You are a new person, with new energy, attracting new people.

> **One of my favorite mantras for this category is: I am a conscious creator, creating a new life, with new rules.**

119

Soul Contracts: Earth is a place to learn, develop, and grow. I believe our soul makes soul contracts with other souls prior to coming to Earth for the purpose of helping each other through this lifetime. We usually make soul contracts with souls we have experienced other lifetimes with. This could be to clear away karma or because we know we can count on a soul to help us grow. A person on Earth may come into your life, break your heart, and trigger your spiritual awakening, not to hurt you, but because it was part of a soul contract to help you grow vibrationally.

I know you're again thinking, "There is no way I made a contract with my narcissistic mother."

Keep in mind, you made a contract with that soul, not that human. A soul may have intended to be a good caregiver, but once on Earth, was influenced by low vibrations and with their free will they may have strayed from the contract. Once a soul contract is fulfilled, or if the other is incapable of completing their part of the contract, they may just fall out of your life. I call this "cosmic cancellation."

> **Comic Cancelation:** The underlying energetic reason why people fall out of our lives. When someone seemingly falls out of your life for "no reason," it is because they're no longer in vibrational alignment with you, have completed their soul contract, or are unable to complete the contract at that time.

I had a group of great friends from kindergarten through high school to the beginning of college. After that, they completely fell out of my life. At first, I was very hurt by this fallout, but then I realized this was cosmic cancelation. There was no actual reason why these friendships fell out of my life, other than our contract ending. I had the best times with these girls throughout my school life, and I could not have imagined it any other way. I loved them like they were my sisters, but ultimately, we fell out of vibration. We served one another for many years, and then it was finally time to go. Instead of letting the end of these friendships kill me, I have found deep appreciation for the times we have had together.

Positive Bitch Tip: I no longer measure friendships by how long they last; rather, I measure them by the depth of the connection in the moment.

They Can't Take Your Power If You Don't Give It to Them

Understanding why we align with certain people and using that knowledge to study ourselves is always helpful. Obsessing over why they left us is not. I'll say this loud so even the people in the back can hear. NOT EVERYONE IS MEANT TO STAY IN OUR LIFE FOREVER AND THAT IS OKAY!

> **Positive Bitch Tip:** Life has the meaning you give it. Give the relationships that have ended a positive meaning instead of a negative one.

I see the friendships that have left my life as a double positive. They not only served me for many years, and I them, but when we fell out of vibration, it showed me my frequency was rising, and so we were no longer in alignment.

If we try to hold onto people who are no longer in vibrational alignment with us, we can stunt our growth and block our blessings. Trying to hold on to lower-vibrational people lowers our vibration. We become the average frequency of the people we hang out with most. Are these lower-vibrational people worth you hurting your own life? NO! This is a waste of time and energy. No one is worth missing out on the life you incarnated here for. It's helpful to write out the relationships that have expired in your life on one side of a piece of paper, and then use the other side to write one to three lessons, realizations, or positive meanings you can derive from those relationships. We tell ourselves many stories; why not tell ourselves a good one?

One Side of the Paper:	Other Side of the Paper:
Friends from childhood	1. Helped me survive elementary and high school 2. Gave me amazing memories 3. Once we fell out of vibration, it showed me I was vibing in a new higher frequency

It's not always easy to just turn off the love you have for another, but that is not what I am asking you to do. You can love others from afar, that's fine. What I want you to do is just lower the volume of love you have for them and raise the volume of love you have for yourself. When we keep trying to hold onto others, obsess about our exes, or allow others to tell us who we are, we start to erode from inside of ourselves. Over time, as we continuously allow mistreatment from others, we further betray ourselves and end up hating ourselves for allowing such treatment. If you cannot let them go for you, let them go for your younger self. That little you has so many dreams and aspirations, and they did not come here to let *Brad* or even *Brittany* block them from their purpose. You have a commitment not only to this current version of you, but to the past version of yourself too.

Self-Love Is a Muscle

I've been the girl that hated herself, and I am the girl who loves herself. I'll give you a hint: One of these is way more fun than the other. I love self-love, but I was turned off by the self-love movement. I didn't understand how to just "love myself." Then I figured out that self-love is not something that falls from the sky and hits us on the head; it's a muscle that we must build.

> **Positive Bitch Tip:** Just as we build up physical muscle, we also must build up psychological self-love muscles. We wouldn't go to the gym one time and expect to have abs, so don't say one affirmation and expect to love yourself. It's a process.

We don't have to love every version of ourselves. I do not love the version of me that was constantly bingeing, hating herself, self-sabotaging her relationship, and was depressed. If someone was treating me the way that version treated myself, telling me terrible things about myself all day, forcing me to shove down my emotions with food, and hurting my relationships, I would not like them at all. I don't have to love that version of me, but I honor and respect the contrast she showed me because she allowed me to clarify and love myself for who I am now. I needed that older version of me to lead me to this updated version of me. I don't love that version, but I thank her. Instead of wasting time trying to love the version of yourself that is hurting yourself, begin to accept where you are at. Thank this version of you for showing you what you do not want for yourself. Thank this version of you for getting you this far. If you got yourself here, you can get yourself out of here, too. You have had the power all this time; today you have become conscious of it. Imagine the things you can do now.

123

Learning You Deserve to Be on Your Pedestal

You did not fall out of God's back pocket and stumble upon Earth. You are here for a reason, your life has purpose, and you are inherently worthy just by being born. The same creator who wanted the ocean to span 70 percent of earth's surface, the sky to encompass the whole planet, the birds and the bees, also thought you were important enough to exist and take up space in this realm. One thing about God, this loving energy does not make mistakes. As humans we mess up a ton, but God, yeah, no mistakes there. Even if your caregivers didn't *intend* for you to be here, God did, and that's why you are reading these words right now. No. Mistakes. God is the ultimate artist, and no artist purposely creates ugliness. I never met a painter, architect, or dancer who told me they wanted to create something ugly. You are beautiful down to your cellular level, and you deserve to feel good. Just because you cannot see that yet does not mean it isn't true. It means your perception is fuzzy.

To build ourselves up, we must accept where we are at. I tried to pretend I didn't binge-eat, I tried the whole false-positivity thing, I tried faking it till you make it, and none of that helped. Being in denial of parts of you will not allow you to release those parts. Pretending you are happy with parts of yourself that you despise will not allow you to change or release those parts either. We don't have to remain the same if we do not love what's in front of us, and we don't have to love what's in front of us to accept what is.

> **Positive Bitch Tip:** We can't hate ourselves into loving ourselves.

124

We can't hate ourselves into being healthy. We can't hate ourselves into success. We can, however, accept where we are at and decide to go in a new, higher-vibrational direction. Accept your current status, whatever it may be. Accepting our current status doesn't mean we are stuck there; it means we are opening ourselves up to new possibilities. By accepting what is in front of you, you are shortening the gap between where you are right now and where you wish to be. Look at the things you do not like about yourself.

❤ **Ask yourself, "Are there actionable steps I can take to change this?"**

If you do not like something like your weight, acne, style, job, lack of coping mechanisms, relationship to self, or low self-esteem, these are all things that can be changed. Begin to get curious about how you can change what you do not like and do research. Make a list of actionable steps you can take. If the current version of you isn't sure what to change, ask the version of you who already has what you currently desire. There are limitless versions of you in this quantum field. This means that, even if the version you embody now doesn't have something you desire, there is a version of you out there that does. If you want something another version of you has, simply ask that version out loud what they did to get those results.

125

❤ **Ask, "What does the version of me that has _____ do to achieve those results?"**

I asked, "What does the version of me that has my desired body do to achieve those results?"

That version of me had new, cute workout clothes she felt great in, worked out six times a week, drank more water, stopped letting herself negatively spiral about her body, practiced gratitude daily, meditated, did yoga, blessed her food before consumption, and addressed her inner child wounds.

You will be shocked at the responses you get. I recommend taking about ten minutes to sit silently to get connected with yourself. Asking is great, but being able to hear the response is another story. You must be connected to yourself to hear the next steps. Once you receive your answer, you can just start doing that thing. Trust yourself. The answers are within you; you just need to ask for them to come to the surface. Instead of complaining about what you hate, begin to turn your attention to what you would love and become inquisitive about how you can get there.

> **Positive Bitch Tip:** Complaining about where you are will never get you to where you want to be. Set your eyes upon a positive place so you can move toward that.

Remember: If you keep doing what you have been doing, you will keep repeatedly manifesting the same results.

126

How to Take Your Power Back from People

To get ALL of ourself onto our own pedestal, we have to accept ourself in all of our glory. Say hello to shadow work.

Your Shadow Self

Let's dive deeper into your shadow self. Your shadow self is made up of the parts of yourself that you think are unacceptable or unlovable. It is ultimately the parts of ourself that we have disowned and tried to hide. These parts may be made up of emotions, personality traits, or thought patterns. As the "can-do" girl, the aspects of myself I thought were unacceptable were laziness, rage, sensitivity, and rebelliousness. Even though I had the capacity to be lazy, I never allowed myself to engage with that trait. Anytime I became emotional, I would immediately try to shove it down for fear of being seen as "sensitive." When I saw these traits in others, it would anger me. What we push down in ourselves, we will dislike or be triggered by in others. This makes us more vulnerable to our outside environment triggering us, therefore controlling us, and hurts our ability to put *all* of ourselves on the pedestal. However, when we claim all the parts of ourselves, even the ones we have deemed unacceptable, this makes us more accepting and understanding of ourselves, as well as others around us. This provides inner peace and safety, which allows for outer peace and safety too.

To find your shadow self, write a list of five to ten things you dislike/ hate in others.

You can use these prompts to help clarify your shadow self:

☾   *Who is someone I dislike and why do I dislike them?*

☾   *What personality traits bother me the most in others?*

☾   *What do I find most annoying about other people?*

If you hate loud, aggressive, nosy people, it's because you reject those qualities within yourself. If you do not allow yourself to engage with those traits, when someone else does you may subconsciously think, "Well, if I don't do that, why should they be allowed to do that?"

Once you have made a list, look at the qualities you wrote down. These are the qualities of your shadow self. To bring this shadow to the light, you must begin to realize that not allowing yourself to express a part of yourself does not mean it isn't there. We are all human, and have a spectrum of characteristics. Destigmatize the characteristics you have hatred for by identifying them within yourself. When we understand the feelings of another because we have experienced them ourselves, it allows us to have compassion for them instead of hatred. We are not just a saint, and we are not just a sinner. We are multidimensional beings with the capacity to experience a whole spectrum of emotions, traits, and thoughts. When we embrace our wholeness, we place ourselves on the pedestal. It's not always pretty, but we are always worthy. Every part of you deserves to be heard, seen, and validated, even if you do not wish to act out those traits daily. Reclaim all of you.

Here are some journal prompts or questions to ponder that will allow you to put all of yourself on your pedestal:

C *When do you feel yourself trying to push down emotions or characteristics?*

C *What emotions or characteristics are these?*

C *Why wouldn't you allow yourself to feel or express these characteristics?*

C *Who told you that you weren't allowed to feel or express these characteristics?*

C *What does that person even know?*

C *When did you feel rejected or ashamed as a child?*

C *How have you rejected parts of yourself as an adult?*

C *What's really so bad about being (insert trait)?*

C *How do you sometimes display these characteristics yourself?*

C *What traits do you let out when no one else is around?*

C *What side of yourself do you not let others see? Why?*

C *How can you express this side of yourself in a healthy way?*

You can even practice tapping into those traits. If you are extremely introverted and never speak up, next time someone cuts you in line, allow yourself to speak up! As long as no harm is done to others, tapping into the parts of you that have been suppressed allows you to understand who you truly are more deeply and is fun to experiment with.

It's never too late to put all of yourself on your own pedestal. So dust that shit off and take your place.

YOU ARE HERE

The second hurdle we must overcome when we are taking our place on our pedestal is pushing everyone else we originally put there off. Don't worry, they'll land on a plush cloud, it's your time, baby! We must address the energy vampires. Energy vampires are those who suck all your energy. Each time we are done talking to them, we feel completely depleted. Energy vampires don't have to be people. Social media and the news are also forms of energy vampires. To place yourself on the pedestal, you must make some room. Every time you feel depleted, I want you to make a note of it. Over time, you will have a list of what is depleting you and will therefore be equipped to notice patterns and triggers.

Once you identify the triggers, you can either avoid them or place a boundary there. If talking on the phone for two hours is draining for you, tell your friends you have other work to do or you are limiting phone time. If social media makes you feel insecure, don't allow yourself to scroll for hours.

130

Positive Bitch Tip: We are created equal, but not everyone or everything deserves our equal attention. We are not slaves to other people, and we will not let them take us on an emotional rollercoaster. It's our life, our pedestal, and our destiny to create. Cutting out or limiting energy vampires in your life allows you to have more energy, time, and space for things that make you feel alive.

The third hurdle is staying on your pedestal. There will be times when others' limiting beliefs that have been projected onto you will pop up and push you off your pedestal. It's our responsibility to pluck these toxins from our pedestal and drain them from our energy field. I used to feel completely uncomfortable going out in public when I had a breakout on my face. I thought I had to go everywhere with makeup on. It was so annoying and felt limiting to me. Then I realized, why am I doing this if it doesn't feel good to me?

I asked myself, "Who made me feel unworthy when I look this way? Is this my own thought? Do I really think I cannot go out in public when I have a breakout?"

Once I confronted the thought, I knew it wasn't mine to begin with. I stopped believing this thought. I stopped feeding it. I kicked It off my pedestal.

Positive Bitch Tip: Interrupt the thoughts that make you feel less-than. Let the thoughts other people fed you starve and die out. They cannot survive if you do not nourish them. Nourish the thoughts you want to feel and see in your life.

Now, when one of those thoughts comes up, I say, "That isn't mine, I'm not going to own that thought."

The fourth hurdle is accepting, letting go of, or forgiving what others have done to us. When we let people from our past control our present, that is letting them on our pedestal. People will hurt us, it's bound to happen, but we will be damned if we hurt ourselves! We hurt ourselves when we allow those from our past to influence us negatively now. Are you really going to let your unhealed ex control your whole life? If they hurt you then, don't let them keep hurting you now. If they couldn't give you what you deserve then, you can give yourself the love, happiness, and joy you deserve in the now. Letting what happened go doesn't mean they won't get what they deserve. Karma's a fellow positive bitch, and she'll take care of it for you. When you give it up to Miss Karma, this allows you to lower the volume of anger, disappointment, and hurt you have for them, and once again raise the volume of love you have for yourself. You are letting it go not even because it's the right thing to do, but because it allows you to free yourself. This isn't about them anymore. They've taken enough of your time, energy, and focus. This is about you taking back your consciousness and building a life you can love.

My favorite way to release people from my pedestal who have hurt me is Ho'oponopono.

> **Ho'oponopono:** An ancient Hawaiian healing modality that literally means "to make right." This technique allows us to take responsibility over our life, our state of being, and our pedestal, ultimately allowing us to take our power back.

This modality allows us to release our past so we may live in our present. Ho'oponopono is four mantras. Say these four mantras out loud.

I'm Sorry
Please Forgive me
Thank You
I Love You

When doing this technique, you can think of someone you hurt, someone who hurt you, or even your past wounded self.

I'm Sorry: Say this to accept responsibility for the energy you have brought to the table and the corresponding events that aligned with you. If you have hurt another, you can envision them in your mind's eye and apologize to them. If you have allowed yourself to stay in unhealthy circumstances, you can say sorry to your past self or your higher self.

Please Forgive Me: Say this to make amends with that other person, your past self, or your higher self for allowing such treatment. You can also ask God for forgiveness if you feel called to, as you and others are both His creations.

Thank You: Say this to raise your vibration and show gratitude for that other person, your past self, or your higher self energetically accepting your apology. You can also thank God, the Universe, your angels, etc., for helping you in releasing this experience. This allows all negativity to be cleared.

I Love You: Say this to further raise your vibration, cleanse yourself of the experience, and set yourself free.

Placing Yourself on Your Pedestal

I have found it is easy to obsess over a partner and put them on my pedestal when I have nothing going on for myself. When I didn't have anything that made me feel alive in my own reality, I looked for happiness in my partner. If you have nothing in your life that gives you the OMG FEELING, meaning you feel alive, present, and happy AF, I recommend you find a hobby. If we do not have activities, hobbies, or anything in our life that fills us up, we will starve for that energy in others. When our partner who used to fill us up leaves, they take our happiness with them.

> **Positive Bitch Tip:** When you're feeling in doubt, ask yourself "WWAPBD?" a.k.a. "What would a Positive Bitch do?"

Here are some of examples of how to be a Positive Bitch, living in Positive Bitch Frequency.

Dating Yourself

If you want to love yourself, you have to get to know yourself. How do you get to know someone else? You have to hang out with them. If you want to discover yourself, DATE YOURSELF.

> **Positive Bitch Tip:** To love thyself is to know thyself.

Dating yourself means, instead of getting under someone new and trying to distract yourself, you get into yourself. Take yourself out on a date, literally. I do this all the time. I've done this while I was single, and I still do it now that I am in a relationship. Dating myself is essential to me staying me! How do you date yourself? This can look different for different people. I take myself to infrared saunas, yoga classes, shopping, restaurants, I try new recipes, I go to the harbor to read, and I love to go on trails by myself. This gives me time to get to know me and explore what I like and what I do not like. If you want to attract someone who is interesting and has things going for them, you will want to also be interesting and have things going for you. Dating myself has allowed me to see that I actually am fun, and I truly enjoy my time with myself.

Use this time to experiment with new hobbies! I never would have found yoga if it weren't for me trying to build myself back up from codependency. In dating myself and trying a new hobby, I have found a new love. Yoga now is something I do multiple times a week, and it makes me feel like I'm on cloud nine. You never know where your self-dates will take you, so take this chance on yourself.

One day you may get married, have children, and never have a moment of peace again. This is your time to soak in that alone time, and get to know you. People will come in and people will go out, but you will always have you. You are worth the investment. You are worth getting to know.

Pick a date, a place, and a time, and take yourself out. Show yourself the love you have been wanting from a partner, and see how your vibration and self-love rises. This is how it feels to be on your own pedestal.

Finding a Strain That Serves You

A strain is something that is somewhat difficult for you to do, but possible. Cardio is a strain for me, and that's why I lovingly encourage myself to do it weekly. I used to think I couldn't run that far, but after deciding to do it anyway, I have proved to myself how powerful I am. Engaging in this activity weekly has made me more confident in other things as well. Now when someone says I cannot do something or there is something I've never done before, I know, if I could run three miles, I can do this too.

Realizing how powerful I was also allowed me to place less importance on my looks. It made me understand that if my clear skin is the best thing about me, maybe I need to get some damn hobbies. I wanted my skin to be clear, but it's also the least interesting thing about me. I am more than my skin, I am more than my looks, I am a goddess, and I should feel like one too. To find a strain that serves you, find something that is difficult, but doable, and start implementing it into your weekly schedule. This will build up your self-confidence, which will help you build self-love.

Some examples of strains include:

+ *Reading*
+ *Writing*
+ *Meditating*

+ *Learning a new skill*
+ *Working out*
+ *Pushing yourself outside of your comfort zone*

Stay True to Your Word

If you say you'll do something, do it. Stop betraying your own word! If you cannot trust yourself, it will be much harder to trust everyone around you. When you stay true to your word, you build self-trust, which will help you build self-love. If you promise yourself that you will start writing that book tomorrow, you better start writing tomorrow! When we betray our own word, we only hurt ourselves. Don't betray your morals, values, beliefs, or thoughts for others, either. Hold yourself up high on that pedestal, and you will find others who either see the world similarly, or can appreciate your differences. Only when you try to fake a persona will you align with people who cannot understand you and/or shame you.

Romanticize Your Life

We often feel the most seen when someone does the littlest thing for us. What if we did the littlest things for ourselves? I find the smallest action of lighting a candle every morning, honoring myself and God, creates the biggest shift for the rest of my day. Having a small cup of tea allows me to write for the longest stretches of time. Cleaning my space for ten minutes leaves me feeling amazing for ten hours.

(*How can you romanticize small moments of your day?*

(*How can you romanticize the space you live in?*

(*What little action can you shift to make a big difference?*

When we use these little moments and make them into something magical, it allows us to be more present. Most of our life may be mundane, so let's put the magic in the mundane and romanticize the little moments, because what is life but a collection of little moments strung together?

Love Yourself to Health

If your parents gave you a really valuable gift, you would take care of it. The most valuable thing God gave us is our bodies and good health. We, however, forget to take care of ourselves all of the time! If we do not have our health, we aren't able to do much. Take care of the vessel you were gifted as part of being human. Eat foods that make you feel good. Drink water. Move your body. This has nothing to do with having a specific body type. This has everything to do with making space for ourselves to feel good in our skin homes! When we take care of our bodies, it naturally raises our vibration and places us on the pedestal. This is self-love in action.

MENifestation 101

The people I had to not just kick off my pedestal but *kickbox* off my pedestal were the men I've dated. It's imperative that we understand how we are using our energy when it comes to dating. We wouldn't play chess with no understanding of how to win a match; we don't want to date with no understanding of how to align with a match either. If we notice our potential partners are repeatedly just "not that into us," ghosting us, or side-*chicking* us, the common denominator is us. No, it's not that you are unlovable or unworthy, or suck; it's that you aren't using your energy in a way that helps you. We have a lot of creative control when we are dating, but if we aren't using our energy in a way that is conducive to our desires, we will not like the results. You can get the partners you want, and radically shift your dating life, but it requires you to shift what you are bringing to the table energetically.

Positive Bitch Tip: We are either standing tall on our pedestal and attracting others, or we are placing others on our pedestal and chasing. It's one or the other, and this makes all the difference.

We put our potential partners on the pedestal when we energetically chase them.

Energetically chasing includes:

+ *Waiting around for their text*

+ *Texting them repeatedly without a reply*

+ *Saying their name countless times a day*

+ *Stalking their social media*

+ *Checking their follower count*

+ *Saying you're "manifesting" them when you're just obsessing over them*

+ *Canceling your prior plans to see them*

+ *Changing your values, morals, or beliefs because you think they'd like you better if you were different*

+ *Liking them better than you like yourself*

+ *Focusing on how they're perceiving you instead of focusing on your own enjoyment*

+ *Thinking they are the ONLY one that could ever possibly be for you*

+ *Calling them your specific person*

Energetically Chasing: Sending another more energy than you are giving to yourself, therefore creating an imbalance in how you are using your own power. Often means living in accordance with someone else's will rather than your own. Energetically chasing will leave you feeling depleted, anxious, needy, codependent, and unfulfilled.

Positive Bitch Tip: Anything that is chased, whether it's a boy or a bug, will run away.

Energetically chasing them is acting as if you are a bowling ball and they are the pins. You'll run them down and repel them in the opposite direction. In a relationship, we want it to be like a tennis match, where you send some energy, and they send some back. You hit, they hit, and so on. It's not really about you or them; it's about how your energy is interacting with theirs. The people we date can feel our energy, and they know when we are sending way too much. When we are pedestaling them, they have no room to miss us because they already are surrounded by our energy. However, when you shift your energy, they will also feel the shift and lean toward you rather than run away.

How can we take our partners off the pedestal and stop chasing?

Normalize the Bare Minimum

Your potential partner texting you back is NORMAL. If they can play video games with NPCs (non-player characters) on their PS5, they can take all of five seconds to text you. If they are the masculine leading individual, they should pay for your dinner. You are paying for your hair, nails, facials, makeup, and so much more. The least they can do is pick up the tab. They should initiate plans with you, they should try to make you feel safe, and they should try to meet your needs. This should not be glamorized. If they cannot seem to do the bare minimum, see this as a TURN-OFF. This isn't a moment for you to try to prove you are worthy of their love; this is a moment for you to see they can't give you what you want. RUN!

140

> **Positive Bitch Tip:** When we feel they are pulling away, our first instinct is to try to give more, but this only repels them further. If giving them some of your energy wasn't appreciated, giving more of the same will not be appreciated either.

Stop Overfeeding Them

Allowing people to not treat you with the utmost respect and love is a symptom of you placing them on your pedestal. What would help is putting them on an energetic diet.

This means: NO MORE SENDING THEM ENDLESS AMOUNTS OF YOUR ENERGY FOR NOTHING IN RETURN BECAUSE YOU ARE NOT A BOWLING BALL.

If you have been overfeeding them with your energy, you're simultaneously starving yourself. Shift your focus and your energy will follow.

When we are chasing them, it's because we are chasing a feeling. There are two questions that will help you shift your focus and get the feeling you want:

❨ *What do you feel when they are around you?*

❨ *How can you find this feeling outside of them and give it to yourself?*

There are more ways to feel loved, appreciated, and seen. It does not only have to come from a romantic partner.

Stop Ghosting Your Own Needs

There is a difference between being needy and expressing your needs. Expressing your own needs places you on the pedestal and communicates to your subconscious mind, as well as the Universe, that you know your worth. There is nothing wrong with expressing your needs; in fact, it must be done if you want a healthy relationship. Newsflash, no one can read your mind!

Being needy is when you place the other person on the pedestal and derive all your happiness, excitement, and love from them. When we are needy of them, we often will ghost ourselves, thinking it's a way to ensure we get them. However, this gets us the opposite of what we want. If you can ghost your own self, why wouldn't someone else? When you ghost your own needs, beliefs, morals, and values, it will be easy for that other person to ghost you too. People will continue to mirror this behavior until you show up differently.

> **Positive Bitch Tip:** How we treat ourselves mentally, physically, and energetically will teach other people how to treat us. If they see that you do not value yourself, they will not value you either.

Have Non-Negotiables

Non-negotiables are self-boundaries that help you stay on your own pedestal. Non-negotiables may include hobbies, activities, rituals, and/or practices that are important to you and allow you to feel your best. Regardless of who comes in or goes out of your life, your non-negotiables stay!

Now that I'm in a relationship, I have the same non-negotiables I had when I was single. Whether or not Mr. Boyfriend is here, I work out six days a week, record a podcast weekly, upload a daily TikTok, go to yoga, meditate, eat what is high-vibe for me, and wear what makes me feel comfortable. Having non-negotiables not only helps me be me and feel good, it also allows me to stay focused on me, rather than obsessing about what he's doing. I can't worry about what Mr. Boyfriend is doing while I'm trying to hold the boat pose. This helped me place myself on my pedestal and see my life from my own point of view, rather than through his gaze.

If you don't have any non-negotiables, date yourself to start finding out more about yourself, what you like, what you don't like, what you value, what you believe in, and what your passions are.

) **Positive Bitch Tip:** Discovering and building yourself up is
(the best work of art you will ever create.

To move on from MENifestation 101 to Mastering MENifestation, we must first look to our Divine Feminine Energy, our forgotten superpower.

6

Positive Bitches Are Magnetic Through Mastery of Their Divine Feminine Energy

Taking Your Power Back from the Masculine Energy

Conscious Question: "Am I Authentically Acting from My Pedestal?"

Who Is She?

Every single person, regardless of gender, is made up of both feminine and masculine energy. While most women lead with their feminine energy and most men lead with their masculine energy, this isn't always the case. Learning how and when to embody each energy is the key to balance and success. Society's programming of hustle culture has greatly affected the way we humans show up. It has pushed many women, myself included, into masculine energy overdrive, leaving us feeling depleted, burnt-out, and with no inspiration. When we are in our masculine energy for too long, we get stuck in our head, become overcontrolling, and very rigid. When we are chasing something outside of ourselves, it is because we are lost in our wounded masculine and need to reintroduce ourselves to our feminine energy.

We can only lead with one of the energies. It breaks down to about a 60/40 split. If I lead with my feminine, I will lead with this energy about 60 percent of the time and lead with my masculine 40 percent of the time. Neither energy is bad, and both are needed at different times. The masculine energy is the structure that the feminine energy flows through. Masculine energy is needed to complete projects, focus, and create stability in our earthly life. Masculine energy is the master of this earthly dimension. When we are too steeped in our masculine energy, we may become rigid and stuck in survival mode, too focused on the 3D. The feminine energy is needed to create, attract, and flow with the Universe. The feminine is the master of dimensions beyond this earth. If we are too steeped in our feminine energy, we may find it hard to complete anything, and can become ungrounded. However, when we marry these energies within ourselves, it allows us to balance our connection with this realm and those beyond.

(Light) Masculine Energy Traits	(Light) Feminine Energy Traits
Doing	Being
Thinking (the head)	Feeling (the body)
External Action	Internal Intuition
Grounded	Trusting
Structured	Flowing
Disciplined	Expressive
Goal-Oriented	Creative
Assertive	Surrendered
Giver	Receiver
Protective	Magnetic
Present	Nurturing

I lead with my divine feminine energy about 60 percent of the time. When it comes to how I live my life, especially how I show up in my relationship with Mr. Boyfriend, I prefer to be in my feminine. I remain on my pedestal, which allows me to attract what I want rather than chase, I allow myself to receive love from others, I am surrendered to my divine plan, and I express my emotions and creativity daily. The other 40 percent of the time, I use my masculine energy for my business, career, and daily workouts. While I love to just "be," I also make sure I hit deadlines, make time for my work, and create goals.

The Other Side

While at my core I lead with my feminine energy, I lived most of my life before spiritually awakening in survival mode. This on top of hustle culture deeply steeped me in my masculine energy. I was constantly looking for the next threat, trying to force my body to look different by undereating which led to bingeing, and avoiding my emotions. When Mr. Boyfriend and I first started dating, I was so in my masculine that I never let him in fully. I never allowed myself to surrender completely or trust him with all my being. I had my masculine shield high up due to past trauma and fear. Anytime he would cry or show emotion, I felt uncomfortable. This had nothing to do with him. I couldn't see other people feel their emotions because I was so out of touch with my own. When we sway too far into one energy, we end up exhibiting the wounded version of that energy. We don't want to be in overdrive, but in balance.

Wounded Masculine Energy Traits	Wounded Feminine Energy Traits
Avoidant	Codependent
Dominating	Feels Powerless
Over Controlling	Manipulative
Forceful	Over-Sensitive
Shoving Down Emotions	Shutting Out Others
Overthinking	Feels Unworthy or Shameful
Unstable	Needy

By healing and activating our feminine energy, we will simultaneously be healing our masculine energy. Healing begins with the willingness to let the past go. When we let our past go, we allow ourselves to step out of survival mode and into the present moment. Only when we stop looking for potential threats can we put down our masculine shield. Many of us put up a masculine shield because we think the feminine energy is weak. We put this shield up in hopes of protecting ourselves, but end up shutting down the power that the divine feminine exudes. While she is nurturing, flowing, and surrendered, she is nowhere near weak. The divine feminine is the creator of all life force. She is the utmost powerful. We do not have to fear leading with our divine feminine, as she is the one who creates all. The feminine energy is represented by the color black or darkness, because all creation begins in darkness.

) **Positive Bitch Tip:** As Positive Bitches, we dance with our
(darkness, we do not run from it.

The masculine energy is represented by the color white.

Healing the Divine Feminine

148

When we are hurt by our divine feminine caregiver, our feminine energy often becomes wounded. This is our first relationship with a feminine energy, so if they hurt us, betray us, or leave us, we will think all feminine energies are like this. We may be so hurt by their energy that we push down the feminine energy in ourselves. Begin to release the anger you have toward this caregiver. You can use Ho'oponopono from the last chapter to do this. You can also practice not allowing this caregiver to take up space on your pedestal. She did the best she could with what she knew. You know better, you will do better, but you will not let her hold you back. Set up boundaries with this caregiver. If she couldn't protect you in the past, you can protect yourself now.

> **Positive Bitch Tip:** It doesn't matter what you allowed then; right now you are someone different. It's never too late to draw a new line in the sand.

When setting a boundary, use first person terms like "I" and "me."

Instead of saying, "**You** suck," "**You** weren't there for me," or "**You** can't speak to me anymore":

Try using "**I**" and "**me**" statements like, "**I** am no longer going to be taking part in this because it does not resonate with **me**," or, "**I** am no longer having these conversations because it's not helpful to **me**."

Instead of triggering their ego and creating a fight, you can draw your line and keep it short.

If our masculine caregiver wasn't around, we most likely said to ourselves, "I don't need him, I'll become my own man." Your feminine caregiver may have even taught you to never to rely on any man, and to instead become your own. They did this because they thought they were protecting you, but this belief may actually be harming you, as it shuts down your feminine energy. When you begin to release the anger and resentment you have toward this caregiver, you are allowing your masculine shield to be put down so you can ascend higher. We must get out of our heads and into our present moment. If we are constantly harping on the past, we are not living a life through our own point of view, but from a POV of the past.

I must admit, I was angry when I realized that I had codependent tendencies. I had to forgive my past so I could forgive myself.

> **You can say aloud or write down, "Mom/Dad/Caregiver, I give myself full permission to forgive you for not knowing better or not being able to teach me better. I forgive myself for _____. I no longer will live this way. I am creating a new life with new rules."**

Allow yourself to feel your emotions. Literally sit and cry if that allows you to release the pent-up tension. While feeling your emotions, validate that what you're feeling is real and you are allowed to release this emotion. Talk to yourself lovingly. Hug yourself through the process. Show up for you, and don't cut yourself off or criticize what you feel. This does not have to be logical; it just has to be released. Nurturing your own emotions activates your feminine energy and allows your masculine energy to balance out. The feminine energy within you will nourish the masculine back to life as you move through your emotions and create a safe space for yourself.

Going to the source of why you may have pushed your divine feminine down, and acknowledging her, allows her to activate. I want you to think about all the times you wanted to cry but told yourself you couldn't, told yourself you had to be stronger, put up a shield, or ignored your intuition. Every time you engaged in one of these behaviors, you shut down the divine feminine within you. If you tell that voice to be quiet enough times, eventually she becomes so quiet you can barely hear her. Part of activating your divine feminine is simply inviting that energy to show up.

Further Tapping into Your Feminine Energy

Once you have awareness that you have been swung too far into the masculine, you also have the power to invite your feminine to the forefront of your being. What does this look like? Inviting your divine feminine to your life can look like lighting a candle when you get home from work because you enjoy the aroma. It can look like showing up as authentically yourself, which lets you place yourself on the pedestal and allows you to just "be." It can even look like accepting a compliment. Attention follows our intentions. Just intending to embody your divine feminine is enough for her to flow into your life.

Instead of "doing" all the time, allow yourself to just "be." Exist with no ulterior motive. Drink tea to drink tea, paint to paint, or sing to sing. When you allow yourself to be, you are tapping into your feminine energy and communicating to your masculine that you are safe to show up as your authentic self. Another way to tap into your divine feminine is to get out of your head and into your body. Move your hips, or do any sort of movement, to get out of your thoughts and into your feelings, into your body. Lean into your creativity. Plugging into your creative juices will help you flow with the present. Anytime I sit down at the piano, or create TikToks, I lose track of time because I am completely present with myself and what's in front of me. When you can enter this flow state, where there is no time, no thing, no worry, no one else, you will know you have tapped into the present moment through the door of your feminine energy.

The Other Her

We've talked about the divine feminine, and the wounded divine feminine, but there is one more side: the dark divine feminine. Both the light divine feminine and the dark divine feminine are healthy energies to engage with.

The dark feminine energy is a part of the feminine we rarely talk about. People often mistake this energy for something "bad," but it couldn't be further from the truth. The dark divine feminine is all of the traits women have been told we are not allowed to have, like rage, ferocity, and sternness. It also covers changing, embracing our sexuality, and choosing our own path. The light divine feminine highlights us as the creator and the dark feminine highlights us as the destroyer. Not a destroyer in a negative way, but a destroyer of all cycles that no longer serve us.

Stepping into your dark feminine is saying, "I am allowing myself to feel whatever it is I need to feel," "I can trust my emotions are telling me what I need to know," and "I am setting a boundary here."

152

You tap into your dark divine feminine when you end cycles that are no longer serving you. You tap into your dark divine feminine when you feel lower-vibe emotions that you've been told are not okay to feel. You tap into her when you express yourself, speak up for yourself, and allow your voice to be heard. Being the "good quiet girl" is being in your wounded feminine. There is nothing "good" about that!

Being in your dark divine feminine means expressing your sensuality with no shame, loving yourself, doing what's best for YOURSELF, and not allowing others to take advantage of you. Embodying your dark divine energy, in a nutshell, means being unapologetically YOU.

These energies are not written in stone. We can tap into the light, and then the dark, then into the wounded, and come back around. You are a multifaceted dynamic being; do not limit yourself. When you need to set a boundary, call on the dark and set a boundary, knowing it is okay to do. When you are enjoying the creative process of life, call on the light, and express yourself. When you are hurting, call on either the light or the dark to help bring the wounded out of hiding to be transformed.

How to Take Your Power Back from Your Masculine Energy & Master MENifestation

I can go anywhere, and I will get compliments from all kinds of people. People come up to me to buy me drinks, compliment my energy, my looks, or my confidence. This wasn't always the case, but once I started tapping into both my light and dark divine feminine energy superpowers, everything changed. I put all of myself on my pedestal, and people began to look up at me. If you embrace both the light and dark feminine energies within you, you will get the same result.

Don't Try Hard, Try Easy

The masculine energy can get stuck in survival mode and overfocused on chasing material goods. The masculine tends to get lost under the guise of the ego, while the feminine knows we are much more than what meets the eye. The feminine energy doesn't try hard because she knows she already has everything she needs within her. When we try "hard" for something, or should I say someone, not only do we begin to energetically chase that thing or person, but we place them on our pedestal. This makes them the "king" and us the "peasant."

> **Positive Bitch Tip:** Anytime we place anything on our pedestal, it's automatically energetically above us, and therefore harder to align with. When we place a person on our pedestal, we end up living according to their law, their rules, and their way. We have gotten lost in trying hard; we have forgotten how easy aligning with like-vibrational people is. Like *naturally* attracts like; you don't have to do much. The one thing you must do is show up authentically as yourself, and leave the rest up to the Universe's electromagnetic field.

155

Ask yourself: "How can I enjoy myself tonight?"

Then simply do that.

I use my light feminine energy to set an intention each time before going out. I state that I will enjoy myself. I nurture these positive thoughts with affirmations to create fun new cycles in my life. Instead of falling prey to codependency, I remind myself that I am a divine creator, and I can create happiness and fun in my own life without having to rely on someone else to do something for me. If we are to rely on someone to buy us a drink or compliment us, we are handing our happiness over to strangers. Do you really want to rely on George over there to make your night? I didn't think so. Instead of expecting a stranger to make my night, which creates an attachment to something outside of myself, I intend to make my own night.

> **Positive Bitch Tip:** Switch out expectations from strangers to intending to have fun with yourself regardless of what unfolds. Not only will you have less anxiety while going out, but your energy will be magnetic.

Use the mantras below to intend to have a great day or night and to magnetize your energy. Feel free to come up with your own too!

156

My happiness is in my control

Fun is my divine right

I am hot, healthy, and whole

I am naturally magnetic

I honor myself as the subject of my own life

I have all that I need within me

I am always attracting all the right people at the right time

I radiate confidence, and people can feel this

It's so easy to have fun in my own skin

High-vibrational people are naturally attracted to me

I deserve to have an amazing night

I look and feel beautiful

I am someone people notice

I am the best I have ever been

What I want is obsessed with me

Everything I want, wants me more

High-vibrational opportunities chase me

I release the need for validation

> **Positive Bitch Tip:** Your power is that no one else is exactly
> you. Even if they try to copy and paste your personality,
> they cannot duplicate your exact energetic signature.
> Walk into every place knowing that you are a goddess, and
> that no one has ever experienced your exact energy. Your
> presence is a gift that you are sharing with others. It is not
> something that everyone will get to experience.

Instead of looking to others to fill you up or make you happy, end
the unneeded dependency by inviting your dark divine feminine to
destroy that mindset. When thoughts come up in relation to needing
someone's validation, interrupt that thought and remind yourself
you are the one responsible for your happiness. We know that, where
our focus goes, our energy will naturally flow. If you are focusing
on trying to get others to like you, all your energy will flow to them.
If you focus on you, liking yourself, and enjoying your own night,
you are quite literally filling yourself up with positive energy, which
attracts people rather than pushes them away.

Grounding Through Messy Makeup Mode

158

The divine feminine exists in and expresses herself through our body,
not our head, where our masculine lives. I used to do something I call
"body bouncing."

> **Body Bouncing:** De-centering yourself from your own life
> energetically by switching your point of view from your own to
> someone else's point of view of you.

Instead of enjoying myself, or even having an inner dialogue about what I was seeing, I would have an inner dialogue about how I thought other people saw me. Let's say I aligned with a man named Brad at a bar. Instead of me having an internal dialogue about what I thought about Brad, I would be trying to pick up on what Brad thought of me. I had no time to even assess whether this was a good or bad match because I was consumed by making sure I was making a good impression.

How can we see red flags in others when we are obsessing over potential red flags in ourselves? This is how we pick the wrong dudes.

> **Positive Bitch Tip:** The egg does NOT swim to the sperm, it's science! The divine feminine does NOT chase the masculine, it's energetic law!

Instead of body-bouncing from your POV to their POV, use your divine feminine to get back into your own body. There are two ways to do this. The first way is to use your light divine feminine to regain connection to yourself, instead of ghosting your own point of view. This is a grounding practice. We have long been told to keep sweet, but I'm telling you, forget that, keep in touch with YOURSELF.

While you're out, pause, and feel into your body by using one or more of your five senses to reground your spirit.

Ask yourself:

- ❤ *What am I sensing right now?*
- ❤ *Who am I talking to?*
- ❤ *What do I see?*
- ❤ *What do I feel?*

- ❤ *What do I hear?*
- ❤ *Am I enjoying myself right now?*
- ❤ *Am I behaving in a way that feels good to me?*

When you check in with one of your five senses, you ground your spirit back into your own body, and regain your perspective. You can then decide how you wish to proceed. Maybe you want to stop the conversation and go dance, maybe you need a bathroom break, or maybe you are perfectly happy where you are. Whatever the answer is, it will allow you to act in a way that grounds you in your own human experience.

The second way to get back into your body is by tapping into your dark divine energy, and activating Messy Makeup Mode.

> **Messy Makeup Mode:** Getting out of your head and into your body by dancing in any way that feels good to you. An act of recentering yourself energetically which magnetizes your energy and takes your power back.

I swear to you, the most people come up to me when I'm dancing like no other. I'm not kidding. I dance like God himself told me to start shaking it. I don't care what it looks like, I don't care how people perceive it, all I care about is that it feels good. When I'm dancing and Messy Makeup Mode is activated, I'm having so much fun I literally cannot even worry about what others think. I'm enjoying myself so much, nothing else matters! I am usually so sweaty it looks like I just walked out of a shower, and my makeup is a mess, hence "Messy Makeup Mode." You would think that when your hair is dripping sweat and your makeup is all over the place that no one would want to come within two feet of you, but this is when I get the most positive attention.

To enter Messy Makeup Mode, stop thinking and start dancing. Let your body just move with the music. No judgment, just movement. When Messy Makeup Mode is activated, there's no shame about how you wish to move. Maybe people are watching, but who cares? This is your life, and you will dance how you want to! Messy Makeup Mode shuts down all image-associated shame women have been plagued with. This mode is about completely embracing your beautiful body and sexuality. Trying to look perfect all of the time places others on the pedestal. Instead of trying to look perfect, you will feel perfectly aligned, which will allow perfectly aligned people to come toward you.

The Dessert Principle

The Dessert Principle will help you understand how to balance your energy if you're out and there is someone you're interested in. When we have a slice of some fabulous-tasting cake, that always leaves us wanting more. However, if we were to binge on this cake, even if it was a *fabulous* cake, it would make us sick. The cake's value does not matter. It could be an expensive cake, or a cheap cake. Too much of ANY cake would cause us to be ill, regardless of its value. Anytime we think of this cake we ate too much of, even the thought of it can make us feel sick. Now apply this to energy.

When you meet someone and you give them a sliver of your attention, connection, focus, energy, personality, and even body, this leaves them wanting more. It also allows you to stay on your pedestal and not lose connection to yourself. However, when you are so nervous about them liking you that you ghost your own morals, beliefs, and values, and give them all of your attention, connection, focus, energy, personality, and body, this will make them energetically sick and repel them. This has nothing to do with your value; it has everything to do with how much energy you're giving out.

> **Positive Bitch Tip:** Frequency over force. Let people get to know your authentic energy, don't force them.

> **The Dessert Principle:** Giving a sliver of your energy will always leave others wanting more. Giving too much of your energy will always repel others in the opposite direction.

How do you know if you are giving a sliver or your whole cake? You know you are giving a sliver when you feel good, you're "being" instead of trying to "do" or "get" something, you're enjoying a conversation but not forcing it, you are being authentic to yourself, you're not manipulating yourself to be a version you think they would like, and you are able to assess what is in front of you. If you feel like you are getting extremely nervous, becoming depleted, having to change yourself so they will like you, and trying to control everything, you are stepping into your wounded energies and giving all your cake away.

The Famous Bag

My mom always used to tell me a story about a famous bag.

She told me, "There was a bag everyone wanted. The rich, the poor, the religious, the non-religious, all cultures, all races, all people from around the world. It was not the most expensive. It was not the most beautiful. It was not the most creative. Do you know why everyone wanted the bag?"

I said, "No, why?"

She said, "Because not everyone could have it. It was a limited edition."

While we are all created equal, our worth isn't always *perceived* as equal based on how much energy we give out to others. That bag was no better than any other bag; however, people still perceived it on a pedestal because not everyone could have it. When we rest into our divine feminine, knowing that we are a limited edition, we are *perceived* as higher in value. When we over give our body, presence, or energy, people perceive us as less worthy, even if that is not true. When people perceive us as less worthy, they really are only mirroring back our beliefs about ourselves.

> **Positive Bitch Tip:** We tend to over-give when we think who we already are is not enough. If we think we aren't good enough, others will pick up on this perception and may believe it too. When we realize that we are a limited edition, that literally no one else has our exact unique energetic signature, other people will pick up on this perception, and will believe it too.

163

The CvC Principle

I often get asked if it's divine feminine of us to go up to men or masculine-leading individuals. I'm here to share the good news: YES, IT IS!

There's nothing wrong with choosing who you want and creating a new cycle; however, chasing puts us back into our masculine. If chasing men worked, I would tell you to do it. If no one has said this yet, let it be known that chasing men does *not* work. The women I witnessed chasing men never stopped chasing them. The men usually accepted the offer in front of them, but when they found an offer they deemed "better," they left. The men didn't have to do anything, so there was no skin in the game for them. The men weren't initially that into those women, and the men never increased their connection enough to the point where it could work.

Instead of chasing, we want to choose.

> **The CvC Principle:** CvC stands for choosing vs. chasing. Choosing is aligned with the divine feminine, while pursuing is aligned with the divine masculine. One can choose the person they desire by making the first move without chasing them.

What is choosing? Choosing is starting a light conversation with someone you find attractive, complimenting them while standing next to them, giving them a smile, and then refocusing back onto ourselves. This opens the door, allowing the other person to know you are interested. One time at a bar I literally went up to someone and said, "Buy me a drink?" and they happily obliged. After this, YOU ARE DONE. Once you have made it clear that you are willing to speak to this person, rejoin your friends on the dance floor, take a bathroom break, or do literally anything else other than glue yourself to them the whole night. This allows them to come to you, chase you, hunt you. They can reside in their masculine, and you can reside in your feminine.

What is chasing? Chasing would be initiating the conversation but then following them around all night, texting them first, not once, but every single day, and putting all your focus on them. Choosing allows you to put yourself on the pedestal, while chasing puts the other person on the pedestal. Choosing is magnetic, and chasing is repellent.

You can choose who you want while staying in your feminine and on your pedestal. Choosing allows what you want to flow to you, rather than you running after it. When you know what you want, so you create an opening for what you want (notice all the "yous" in there), this maintains your place on the pedestal and allows the masculine energy to step up and chase you.

Capable Cat Principle

The Capable Cat Principle will help you understand your own motivation for chasing.

Have you ever asked a cat to bark? Probably not, because you know they are not capable of it.

If I told you I asked a cat to bark but it wouldn't bark, you would tell me, "The cat didn't bark because it is not capable of barking."

If I then told you I *needed* this cat to bark for me to feel worthy, validated, and loved, you would ask me, "Why do you need that cat to bark for you to feel worthy, validated, and loved?"

You would tell me, "The cat's capabilities have nothing to do with your worth. Why are you placing your happiness in this cat's hands?"

Now let me ask you, have you ever repeatedly asked, even begged, someone for better communication, for them to stop cheating on you, or respect you? Chances are, probably. See where I'm going with this? If you have repeatedly made your needs clear, and they have not listened or been able to meet those needs, it's not because you are unworthy; it is because they are not capable.

> **The Capable Cat Principle:** If a cat was capable of barking, it would. If they were capable of giving you what you want and need, they would. This has nothing to do with your value as a human, but with their own inability.

Spiraling about why they cannot show up for you leads you into your wounded masculine and right off the cliff of your pedestal. We must stop telling ourselves that we are worthless and unlovable because other people aren't capable of meeting our needs. Embodying our divine feminine means that we know we are inherently worthy, regardless of others' ability to see our value. Instead of asking ourselves why we aren't good enough, we must flip the script.

The Flipped Script Principle

Mixed signals are the worst because they leave room for us to make up stories about how that individual is "trying." Mixed signals are a signal. No communication is communication. Silence speaks volumes. When a masculine leading energy is all about you, you will know. They will want to text you, call you, and ensure they see you consistently.

> **Positive Bitch Tip:** Don't fill in their silences with excuses for them. When someone is truly into you, you won't have confusion, you'll have courtship.

Allow their actions to show you who they are.

Them *not* texting you repeatedly is as deliberate as them texting you. They are either choosing to communicate with you or choosing to ignore you. No one is so busy that they cannot take a couple of seconds to write a short "I miss you" text. Instead of us assuming that maybe they just aren't for us, we often fixate on how their inconsistency is our fault. The only thing wrong with us is that we think there is something wrong with us because a connection isn't "working" the way we thought it should. We end up telling ourselves it's because we aren't pretty enough, good enough, or smart enough, when really, it's one of two reasons.

1. That person simply is not for us.

2. We are energetically chasing them, and we need to rebalance our energy, and tap back into our feminine energy.

Don't try to figure out someone who can't even figure out themselves. When we try to chase an answer that is beyond even that person's understanding, we throw ourselves into a downward spiral of masculine energy, misery, and madness.

If this is happening to you, I invite you to flip the script.

The Flipped Script Principle: Asking yourself the wrong questions will never lead you to the right answers. Instead of assuming they are better and asking yourself, "Why aren't they into me?" assume the best about yourself and ask, "Why do I want someone who isn't showing me affection?" Change the subject of your sentence from "they" to "I," to stop being the object of your own sentence.

Instead of Asking Yourself:	Ask Yourself:
Why aren't they into me?	Why do I want someone who isn't showing me affection?
Why are they so inconsistent?	Why am I attracted to and accepting inconsistency?
How can I make them love me?	Why am I trying to prove myself worthy of love?
Why don't they see my worth?	Why do I like someone who cannot see my worth?
Why do they keep doing this to me?	Why do I keep allowing this behavior?
Why aren't I good enough for them?	What if I'm actually too good for them? Maybe I have higher standards and want more?

Instead of hurting yourself for no reason, reclaim being the subject of your own life, and claim your pedestal. This will lead you back into your own body, self-discovery, and healing.

The Magic of Calling Your Power Back

The most powerful way to embody your divine feminine energy, and master MENifestation, is to call back your power. If you have energetically chased someone, it's never too late to shift your energy and therefore reality. This is a meditative practice for energy recalibration. For this practice, you will have to focus on your sacral chakra. A chakra is a point on the body where energy collects. You can think of it as an energy vortex. While we have many chakras throughout our body, there are seven main chakras that align our spine.

CROWN CHAKRA - VIOLET
CROWN OF HEAD

THIRD EYE CHAKRA - INDIGO
BETWEEN EYEBROWS

THROAT CHAKRA - BLUE
BASE OF THROAT

HEART CHAKRA - GREEN
HEART REGION

SOLAR PLEXUS CHAKRA - YELLOW
BETWEEN NAVAL AND END OF RIB CAGE

SACRAL CHAKRA - ORANGE
RIGHT BELOW BELLY BUTTON

ROOT CHAKRA - RED
BASE OF SPINE, NEAR TAILBONE

If one of these chakras is out of balance, it can cause physical, emotional, and spiritual disturbances. For the sake of this exercise, let's focus on the first two chakras. The first chakra that develops is our root chakra, which is at the base of our spine. The root chakra is represented by the color red. The mantra associated with this chakra is "LAM," pronounced L-U-M, like the word *hum*. You can think of your root chakra and chant LAM to activate and begin to heal this chakra This is responsible for us feeling safe and grounded while on Planet Earth. While this chakra is developing, we are still a baby and do not differentiate ourselves from those around us.

As we grow, the second chakra we develop is our sacral chakra, which is right below our belly button. The sacral chakra is represented by the color orange. The mantra associated with this chakra is "VAM," pronounced V-U-M, like the word *hum*. You can think of your sacral chakra and chant VAM to activate and begin to heal this chakra. As this second chakra is developing, it aids us in understanding that we have a separate perspective from those around us. We know that we are not the same person as our mother, for example, and we are able to differentiate ourselves from others. This is our first step into independence.

This chakra is responsible for our sexual and creative energy. Sexual energy *is* creative energy. We literally create life using sexual energy. I see our sacral chakra as the powerhouse center because it's what allows us to see the world from our own point of view. If the development of our sacral chakra is disturbed due to inconsistent attention, an absent caregiver, or various other traumas, our sacral chakra may be negatively affected and left unbalanced. This can lead to codependency, people-pleasing, loneliness, fear of abandonment, and feelings of anxiety and depression.

I've had thousands of people around the world contact me to tell me that just using the mantra I'm going to give you helped them completely shift their energy to a higher-vibrational state. They felt empowered, fulfilled, and balanced immediately. A side effect, which some people aim for, is that the person they call their power back from ends up contacting them within minutes of using the mantra. When you call your power back from your ex, your boss, whomever, they will feel this, and their relationship to you will shift.

> **Positive Bitch Tip:** Someone cannot miss us if we never stopped energetically chasing them. When you call back your power, you end this chase.

The person you called your power back from will notice this shift and may want to feel your energy again, thus they reach out. If you call your power back just so this person texts you, you may not get any results. That is placing them on the pedestal and still energetically chasing them.

If you call your power back so they cannot harvest your energy, so you can feel fulfilled, whole, and amazing in your own skin, that side effect of them feeling the shift will happen. When it comes to manifesting a person, most people say they're manifesting but really, they're just chasing. Instead of wasting your time sending the other person energy by scripting about them, just call your power back and they will be drawn toward you naturally.

The mantra is: "I lovingly and peacefully call all of my power back to me now." In addition to this mantra, visualize your white light energy leaving their body, through the top of their head, and going into the top of your head, all the way down to your sacral chakra. You can visualize the white light energy like a beam, liquid, or like slime oozing out of them.

The Meditative Practice

 The following meditation is also available in audio format, which can be accessed by QR code.

You can just say the mantra and do the visualization, or you can create a ritual out of this practice to deepen your connection to your sacral chakra. I recommend making this a ritual if you are having trouble focusing on the mantra and the visualization. Setting aside time and creating a sacred space will help your mind to relax and your attention to come into focus. If you wish to make this a ritual, you can light candles, palo santo, sage, or burn incense, but you do not need any of these things. I also recommend doing this in nature, as nature helps us connect back to ourselves.

To begin the meditative practice, find a quiet, comfortable place where there will be no disruptions and no distractions. You can sit or lie down, just make sure that your spine is straight. Have your palms facing upwards, ready to receive your energy. Take an inhale through your nose and exhale through your mouth. As you tune into your breath, you can gently close your eyes.

To anchor into the present moment, do a body scan. All this means is that you will bring your awareness to your body. Begin at the tip of your head and explore how your body feels in this present moment, all the way down to the tips of your toes. Where do you feel relaxation? Where do you feel tension?

For your next inhale, breathe in the present moment and exhale any tension from your body. Repeat this as many times as necessary to feel comfortable in this moment. If your mind starts to wander, use your breath to anchor your focus back onto your body.

172

Bring your attention to your mind's eye. Visualize the most beautiful place in nature you have ever seen or wish to see. Imagine yourself there now. This might be a beach on a tropical island, a park in your favorite city, or maybe a lake you used to spend your vacations near. Get acquainted with this space. Use your senses to feel the heat of the sun or the sand between your toes, or maybe to see a butterfly fly by.

This will be your safe space for this meditation. In this space, nothing can hurt you.

Your sacral chakra is an orange energy vortex that lives right below your belly button. To begin to restore the balance in this energetic center, take your dominant hand and gently tap on the area right below your belly button to activate and turn on your sacral chakra.

As you are tapping on the sacral chakra, chant the mantra associated with this chakra, "VAM." Using your own vocal cords and chanting the associated mantra "VAM" will further awaken your sacral chakra energy.

Do this for a total of six chants.

While you are enjoying this safe space, you see someone starting to walk toward you. This person means no harm. But as they walk closer, you realize this is someone who you feel you have given your power away to. This is someone you feel you've had an uneven energetic exchange with. Maybe they are your ex, your boss, your current partner, or a sibling. Whoever this person is, you feel hurt by them, and you feel like they have more power over you in this current moment. If you feel this way, the truth of the matter is, no one can take your power away from you. You can only willingly give it away. If you can willingly give it away, it means you also have the power to take your power back from them.

Looking at this person, use "The Calling Your Power Back" mantra a total of three times: "I lovingly and peacefully call all of my power back to me now."

Each time you call your power back, you see your white light energy leave their body from the top of their head, and enter into the top of your head. Your white light energy travels down your spine and goes all the way down to your sacral chakra, flooding it with energy. The white energy in your sacral chakra begins to whirl clockwise.

The energy in your chakra is being restored and rebalanced. Your sacral chakra further activates each time, growing larger and brighter in an orange color.

You may feel pulsing, heat, vibration, or nothing at all.

After repeating this process three times, you notice that the person across from you looks dull. They are no longer harnessing your energy. You did no harm to them, but took back what was rightfully yours.

Looking at them, you say, "I release you and set myself free."

They leave in any way that is natural for them to do so.

As you look down at your hands in your mind's eye, and you look down at your legs in your mind's eye, you notice that you actually have a glow around your whole entire being. You're standing in your power and you feel better than ever. You feel at ease. You feel confident, you feel fulfilled, you feel at home, because you are home. You have all of your power anchored back into your sacral chakra. You have successfully called your power back and tuned your sacral chakra.

174

Fail-Safe

If you are having trouble getting your desired result of either someone contacting you or feeling fulfilled, stand up, shake your body out, and clap your hands five times and say, "I am calling my power back to me for me."

This will help you get out of your head, and into your body and shake up any resistance. Repeat this until you feel empowered to try again.

Do not tell yourself, "It just doesn't work for me."

If you say it won't work for you, it won't. You may have been energetically one way for your whole life, so it may take more than saying a mantra once to shift your entire energetic signature. Please be patient with yourself. Take a rest and try again the next day if you feel resistance building up or do not get results. You will shift if you give yourself space to do so.

7

Positive Bitches Catwalk Their Way Through Change, They Do Not Stagnate

Taking Your Power Back from Change

*Conscious Question:
"Am I Fighting or Flowing
Through This Transition?"*

Fearing Change

Every time I experienced change—becoming single, graduating college, or a simple change in routine—it always plagued me with discomfort. Change always felt like trying to walk against the wind with a full face of makeup and hair. You know that treacherous moment when your hair blows into your lipstick and then drags your lip color all over your face to the point where you look like the Joker. You can taste your hairspray because your hair is fully in your mouth. Oh, and the really fun part is you can barely see, as your eyelash extensions are hitting your pupils due to high-speed winds. Overall, not a fun experience.

This is how I viewed change, because I wasn't doing change right. I was moving through change from my ego. Many of us feel a resistance toward change, even when this change is good for us. The tricky thing with our ego is that familiarity tends to feel good, even if that familiar person, circumstance, or place isn't good *for* us. If we want to move through change, we must become more than just our ego, we must become Positive Bitches. Positive Bitches know that, paradoxically, the only thing definite and unchanging is change itself. There is more certainty in change than there is in anything else. Change will always be the backdrop in our life, and we can find comfort in this. I believe in the Universal Law of One, which states that we are one with everything. While physically we look separate through the guise of our ego, spiritually and energetically, we are all connected.

The Law of One: All things exist as one, divinely connected.

We are connected to nature, to each other, to our past self, and our future one. Just as nature has seasons, so do we. We can rest knowing that, no matter how cold it gets in the winter, the summer will come again. We can rest knowing no matter how much the humidity messes with our hair, the crisp air will come again. We can rest knowing that the sun will rise and fall each day. We can rest knowing the moon will shift through all its lunar phases, so why can't we rest when it comes to personal changes that happen in our own life?

> **Positive Bitch Tip:** The seasons of nature operate in a cyclical fashion, and so do we. Life isn't a linear process of start and finish, begin and end, or life and death. We can start, finish, and then start again the next day. We can begin a project, end it, then begin again with a sequel. We live and then die to ourselves many times, constantly being reborn as a new evolved version of ourselves. We have seasons that sway toward socializing and seasons that sway toward isolation, seasons of happiness and seasons of sadness, seasons of change and seasons of being still.

178 We think we want nothing to change, but if everything were to stay exactly the same as it is for the rest of your life, would you really be happy? Would it actually feel good if you had to wear the exact same outfit, eat the same food, see the same people, have the same routine, say the same words, and think the same thoughts? Too much of the same would be dreadful, and it would leave us very bored.

> **Positive Bitch Tip:** Even if we have some fear around change, on some level, we also *want change.*

Creating a Relationship to Change

Resisting change is what causes us pain. Trying to swim against the current of life can feel like you are drowning because no matter what you do, the current is going in the direction it wants to. You can kick and scream, and attempt to swim against it, but the current will persist. The more you try to swim against it, the more tired, breathless, and anxious you become. Trying to fight against what is unfolding in our lives causes us frustration, sadness, anxiety, and depression. When we let go of fighting change, and instead create a relationship to change, it allows us to live peacefully.

You've probably heard the quote, "All suffering comes from desire," which is supposedly said by the Buddha. I'll never forget the day one of my spiritual teachers taught me that this sentence was actually mistranslated because it isn't a literal translation, meaning word for word. This quote that is often put on posters, our backgrounds, and used in speeches is not what the Buddha actually said. A closer translation to what the Buddha actually said is, "All suffering comes from wanting something to be different than what it is."

Too many of us are trying to control too much, and it's causing us to self-destruct. You can have desires, you can have big dreams, you can have whatever it is you want, but you don't need to destroy yourself in order to get there. The thing that so often needs to change isn't our external circumstance, but rather how we are perceiving and showing up in the circumstance. Understanding the Law of Polarity can help us shift our perception to change, allowing us to show up with a new set of eyes.

> **The Law of Polarity:** Everything has an equal opposite in this world, and this is what allows balance. All things have two poles, meaning good and bad, light and dark, happy and sad, love and hate, and so on. This law also means that as deeply as we feel one pole, we will feel the other. As deeply as we feel pain, we will also feel pleasure, and vice versa.

We can create a relationship to change by appreciating what's in front of us while it's there. If you are going through a painful season, know that this is temporary, it will pass, and you will one day feel pleasure just as deeply as you are feeling this pain. If you are feeling pleasure, enjoy it, live it up, and be present, because eventually this season will pass too. If something is unraveling in your life, to the point where you cannot roll it back up, let it unravel.

> **Positive Bitch Tip:** Changing may be hard at times, but trying to resist changing is harder.

In Between Seasons

As we die to new versions of ourselves and continuously evolve, there may be some moments when you aren't the person you used to be, but also aren't quite the next version of yourself either. You're not alone in feeling like this. This was a feeling I've had many times, and what no one told me was that I would mourn the older versions of myself, even though I didn't resonate with that version anymore. There would be times when Old Version CiiCii would've enjoyed what all her friends enjoyed, but the Transitioning CiiCii didn't feel like it resonated with her anymore. I wished I could just go back to the older version of myself and be "normal" with my friends, but I knew that wasn't for my highest good.

There will be seasons when you are dangling in the unknown, and I know it can feel very unsettling, but I invite you to just give yourself the space to grow into the questions you have about yourself. There's a literary device called "dramatic irony" that many writers use. This is when the audience knows more than the characters in the script do.

I often scream at the TV, "If you only knew what I know, you wouldn't do that!"

Mr. Boyfriend frequently reminds me, "If the characters knew what we know, there wouldn't be a show."

The best stories are the ones with a damn good narrative arc. No one wants to watch a movie about a perfect girl living in a perfect world. We want the drama, or as I call it, the contrast!

> **Contrast:** Things we perceive as "drama," "not going our way," "not good," or "frustrating." Even if we perceive a circumstance as such, contrast actually allows us to more clearly understand what we don't want, so we can clarify what it is we do want. Contrast is helpful for us to have a deeper understanding of our true desires and aids us in gaining spiritual muscles.

It's what makes not only movies interesting, but our life too. The characters not knowing everything is what allows them to become curious, grow, and transform. If we knew everything, what would be the point of anything? Seasons of unknowingness are seasons that present growth. When we come into the world as babies, we aren't scared of everything. We look at the world with a sense of wonder. Let's apply that to seasons of uncertainty. Instead of seeing uncertainty as scary, see it as wondrous, exciting, and adventurous. This will make all the difference.

Seasonal Addiction

Sometimes we get emotionally addicted to the seasons, people, or places in our life because of the chemicals we release in relation to them. The more we feel an emotion, the more we condition that emotion in our body. This means the more we feel an emotion, the better we get at experiencing it, and the better our body gets at remembering how to feel it. For most of my life, I was addicted to anxiety. When my boyfriend left my house, I would get anxiety. When I went to class, I would get anxiety. When I had a test, I would get anxiety. When I posted something on Instagram, I would get anxiety. I could be doing pretty much anything, and chances were, I had anxiety.

At this point, I had conditioned my body to feel so anxious that the smallest trigger could set me off. Anxiety gave me something to do. When my boyfriend left, my chest would immediately tighten, and I would play scenario after scenario in my head of him cheating on me. Why? I'd felt anxiety so many times my body already knew instinctively what to do, plus having anxiety allowed me to feel a sense of control. I didn't like thinking of my boyfriend cheating, but it allowed me to think of a multitude of escape plans. I can't repeat this enough: we do not do anything for shits and giggles. My anxiety was giving me the payout of feeling in control. While my body was addicted to releasing cortisol and adrenaline, I was mentally addicted to having pseudo-control.

When we have certain addictions, it's because they are fulfilling some wound or some need. In this case, my addiction to anxiety was fulfilling my need for certainty. If I could think of every possible

182

outcome, I could also think of every possible response to each outcome. I was preemptively trying to protect myself from any potential hurt. This wasn't real control. This was an attempt to create safety by stepping into my wounded masculine.

I decided to start gaining connection to myself, which would then allow me to have better control over myself. Since our mind cannot tell whether we are feeling anxiety or excitement, due to the body releasing similar chemicals for both feelings, I started to tell myself I was excited. Excited that things were changing and changing for the better. Excited, I could show up in a more relaxed way that was closer to my truth. Instead of feeling the tightness in my chest, and then allowing that to trigger anxious thoughts (which would cause further tightening), when I felt the sensation, I started to claim it was excitement. Instead of spiraling about possible future scenarios, I would call my power back after he left, I would do a face mask, and I would use any leftover energy to create. I couldn't change the fact that we could not be together 24/7, but I could change how it would affect me.

Changing How We Fulfill Our Needs

We can either fulfill our needs through healthy behaviors or through unhealthy ones, but you can bet we will fulfill our needs. We can get our need for control fulfilled by celery juice, ensuring health, or a cigarette, ensuring sickness, but either way, we are in control.

- 💜 *Ask yourself, "What emotion or state of being do I feel most of the time?"*
- 💜 *"What need does this fulfill?"*
- 💜 *"How can I fulfill this need in a positive way?"*

Instead of reenacting my usual attachment map response, I took a conscious cab to a new destination. The reason questioning myself helped is because it interrupted the pattern of my conditioned bodily response. Instead of jumping straight to my rehearsed emotions and usual bodily chemical cocktail, I would pause to create a new pattern, one that aligned with my values, rather than one that just fulfilled a need. Our needs override our values; if we want our values and needs to align, we must take conscious control over the conditioned responses that seep out from our subconscious mind.

I no longer fulfilled my need for control through him; rather, I filled it by connecting to myself.

> I affirmed daily, "I can't control every change, but I can control the direction of my change. I choose to change in a positive direction, to make things better and brighter. This feels good."

184

Seasons Passed

It's easy to romanticize a season *after* it's over. An ending of a job, relationship, a change of location, etc., can cause us to move into our sympathetic nervous system if that end was unwanted. Let's say you go through a breakup. This may trigger inner child wounds that relate back to the caregiver you craved love from the most. The pain of a breakup is so intolerable because it's hitting on more than the present breakup wound. When we go through a breakup, we are hitting on wounds we've had since we were a child. Every feeling of abandonment, unworthiness, loneliness, floods our being once again.

These difficult emotions we felt as a child are still within us, they do not just go away. The pain we are experiencing may be triggered by our ex, but it is pain that has been within our bodies since way before our ex ever stepped into the picture.

We naturally want to end this pain, and our mind may tell us the fastest way to do this is to get back with that ex. We then tend to romanticize that partner or season and magically forget all they did that we didn't like because we think it will soothe the pain. This pain is not a green light to get back together with your ex; rather it is a green light to discover, nurture, and love yourself.

It's natural for people to flow in and out of our lives. It's okay to feel sad when people leave our life, it's okay to mourn an older version of yourself, but it's not okay to stay stagnant. Have you ever smelt stagnant water? Well, it stinks! Turns out, when water is still, it smells bad. It's the same thing with energy. When we try to make man-made seasons of still energy, it stinks. Water is meant to move, and so is energy. Instead of stagnating, we want to make room. It's like an overflowing closet of clothes. You cannot buy and fit any more clothes in your closet until you clean out what's already there. Same thing with energy. You cannot call in a new person, place, or opportunity if you do not let go of what is already there and not serving you.

To stop romanticizing your past, every time you think of it in a romanticized way, write down two to three reasons/memories that were not positive. If I were to romanticize my ex, I would write down on a piece of paper two reasons why it could never work.

1. He didn't want kids.
2. He gaslit me always.

Look at this paper every time you begin to romanticize to show yourself a picture that's closer to the truth.

Taking Your Power Back from Change

Things often fall apart so your life can shift into place. When our life looks like it's falling apart, it is shifting so that it can make space for new energy to come in. Before my life flipped upside down, I prayed to God asking for my purpose to be revealed. When I got a terrible breakup, I thought something must have gotten lost in translation. While I knew everything was unfolding divinely, I didn't see how that would lead to my purpose. We don't realize that when we ask for "confidence," "love," "our dream career," and "abundance," those things don't fall from the sky; they come through the doors of change.

> **Positive Bitch Tip:** What we experience as change is opportunity in disguise.

We think that, if we do not get exactly what we asked for in the exact shape and size we imagined, we aren't being blessed. At first, I thought my breakup was the worst thing that could happen to me, but it ended up being the best blessing possible. My breakup was the road to my purpose. I needed to go through that pain and learn about myself and my partner to have a deeper understanding of humanity. I needed that space to spiritually awaken and find myself.

Positive Bitch Tip: Problems are our pushers, and they push us toward our desires. There is great potential in our problems because they force us to look for solutions, and in those solutions, we find what we've praying for. Instead of being used by your problems, take your power back from them, and use them to lead you to what you yearn for.

We know we can't pray for muscles, and hope they'll drop out of the sky. To build muscles, we push and pull weights, put in effort, and use our time. With our spiritual muscles, we must also do some pushing and pulling, even some flowing, and walk through our problems to end up on the other side, where our solution lies. When we ask for something, we are given an opportunity through change to build the "confidence," "love," "our dream career," and "abundance."

Think about some of the "worst" days or circumstances of your life, and reflect on how those days or circumstances pushed you to learn, develop, or grow.

Did that breakup kill you, or lead you to love yourself?

Did failing that subject ruin your life, or lead you to your true passion?

Did getting fired force you to fall apart, or force you to go after your heart's desires?

When you start to see how what you go through is what you grow through, you can ease up the next time you sense change coming your way. Instead of associating change with pain, you can associate change with positive opportunities for growth. Remember, everything is temporary, including seasons of change.

187

Fighting vs. Flowing

I am a natural-born fighter. Living and fighting are synonymous to me. I thought I could fight forever, but let me tell you, it will catch up with you if you do not balance yourself out. I fought every day of my breakup. I fought to reconnect, fought to make myself forget everything I was hurt by, and fought to push down the voice that said I needed time to be alone.

One day I told God, "I just can't fight like this anymore."

What I heard next astounded me.

I heard God say, "Then stop fighting."

It's as simple as that. If you are tired of fighting, stop. When it comes to change, we can either fight or we can flow. Fighting is draining, but flowing is rejuvenating. Fighting means trying to control things outside of ourselves, while flowing means surrendering to the current season.

188

Anytime I feel frustrated, I ask myself, "Am I fighting or flowing?"

To switch from fighting to flowing, we need to build a bridge of surrender. If I feel I am in a perpetual fight, I will recite a couple of surrender-and-support sentences out loud to get myself out of my head. I imagine I'm talking to God, the Universe, my angels, really any being of highest-vibrational truth and love. I set this sentence up by beginning with *surrendering* and then asking for *support*. It looks something like this:

> "God, even though I am feeling uncomfortable and confused, I know that I am always being supported. I surrender to my current circumstance and give it up to you. I will no longer worry about what I cannot control, or what I do not yet understand, as I know it will be taken care of for me. I ask for discernment and clarity in this moment so that I may know how to move forward in a way that is for my highest good."

By interrupting this pattern of fighting, we release this low-vibrational energy instead of building upon it.

When I am flowing, I will appreciate my current state by affirming it.

189

> "I love how good it feels when I am plugged in and connected to myself. I enjoy being a conscious creator.
>
> It's fun to be alive and live in the moment. I am flowing with life, feeling good, and vibing high."

Acknowledging and expressing gratitude for when we are flowing aids in raising our frequency because it puts our focus on the "good," which attracts more "good."

When to Fight

Don't get me wrong. There will be times when it's necessary to stand up and kick some ass, but if you're always fighting, you will burn yourself out. A Positive Bitch is connected to herself and knows when it's time to fight or flow. We are always striving toward balance. If you're constantly fighting, trying to keep your head above water, introduce some flowing. If you're constantly flowing, but can't seem to go in the direction you want, introduce some fight.

There have been many times in my life, and there will be many more, when I have fought to study harder, run longer, learn more, and get back up again. I wouldn't trade those moments for anything. Those are valuable because they allowed me to push past who I thought I was and what I thought I could do. I don't only "flow" and I don't only "fight." I pick and choose my battles, so I don't have to live perpetually on the battlefield.

190

When do I fight?

I fight until I know I've used up everything God has given to me. I fight for my health by doing everything in my control to make it the best it can be. The rest I give up to God and let flow. I fight for my relationship by showing up as the best partner I know how to be. The rest I give up to God and let flow. I fight for my dreams by working daily to create content to help others. The rest I give up to God and let flow.

I make sure I use up all my resources, and then some. Give yourself a chance to show yourself how powerful you are. When you cannot go on any longer, or when you feel you're in a cycle of fighting, surrender, and flow.

Breakups to Birth

Breakups are not failures; they are bridges to new seasons and a new you. I truly believe that breakups are one of the best ways to rebirth a new version of yourself. Once a partner becomes an ex, the space they took up in our life goes on SALE and we get to fill that space with something new. Instead of mourning over the empty space, become curious about what you can fill it with. If you're not sure how to fill up this time, date yourself! Date yourself with the intention of finding out who you are and what you like.

Getting Your Brain on Board

You're probably wondering how you handle the nonstop thoughts about them. As always, I got you. Breakups are weird on Planet Earth because once you break up with your ex physically, you also must break up with them neurologically and energetically. While you may logically understand that this person is no longer in your life, you still have neurological pathways that were created in relation to your ex. Your brain is still looking for your ex's touch, kiss, and presence. When you're triggered into wanting that touch or kiss, and that ex isn't there, your body freaks out trying to get its usual dopamine hit. What our body is really wanting isn't our ex, but a way to get dopamine. We must lead ourselves down new neurological paths to get our dopamine. It's time to get your brain on board with your breakup.

The Fifteen-Minute Rule

Your brain is going to want to bounce back to memories of your breakup as it searches for dopamine. A way to break this habit of thinking of your ex is to employ the fifteen-minute rule.

> **The Fifteen-Minute Rule:** A tool to interrupt thought patterns that are no longer serving you. When you have an undesirable thought, or are stuck in a thought spiral, pause and refocus on something else for fifteen minutes.

When I would get lost in anxious thoughts about my ex or wanted to text him, I would pause, look at the clock, and refocus on any other activity to get my mind off of him. Sometimes I practiced yoga for fifteen minutes, sometimes I found a new recipe that night for dinner, sometimes I read a book, and sometimes I listened to a TED Talk. Whenever I refocused on something else, I ended up forgetting I was thinking of him in the first place. A lot of going through a breakup is just ending the habit of connecting with them by creating a habit of reconnecting with yourself.

192

If after fifteen minutes you still are thinking about them, do another fifteen minutes and see where it takes you. You most likely will forget about them, because it's not really about them. This part of the breakup is actually more about how your brain is currently wired to think *about* them.

Pretend They Are Dead

Positive Bitch Tip: If you want to get over them, pretend they're dead.

No, I'm not kidding. Don't worry, this will not manifest anything negative for them or you. It's only a thought exercise to interrupt your current neurological networks. You are not visualizing them, details about this event, or assigning any emotions to that outcome. You are just using three words to stop yourself from negatively spiraling. This is harsh for a reason. The word "dead" is so shocking that it really makes our brain pause, which gives us time to jump into a conscious cab that will drive us to a new neurological destination. Instead of arriving at the same negative thought spiral, we can begin to refocus on ourselves.

When you think of your ex right now, it's easy to then worry about what they're doing, who they're talking to, if they're getting married, etc. Spiraling isn't helping you because it's trapping you into creating more thoughts about them, strengthening the neural networks you created in relation to them in the first place. You are wasting precious time thinking about someone who has nothing to do with you at this moment.

When you think of them, I want you to immediately interrupt this neurological pathway and say, "Oh wait, they are dead!"

The more you interrupt this thought, the less it will pop up, and the easier it will be to not think about them.

Instead of obsessing over them, you can refocus on you. Place your attention on that hobby, skill, work, school, or whatever else it is you wish to feed your energy to, as long as it's about you and not them.

Trigger Word

If pretending they're dead isn't your jam, I recommend using their name as a trigger to wire in a new healthy behavior. Every time you think of them, use that thought as a reminder to go for that walk, make lemon water, stretch, do breathwork, or whatever other healthy behavior you wish to start incorporating in your life. Every time my attention went to my then ex, I used it as a reminder to read. I read many, many books during our breakup. It was helpful as a healthy distraction, but also allowed me to learn a lot about myself and this world.

Soul Ties

If you feel that your ex has a pull on you, it may be because you have created a soul tie, or energetic cord to them. We all create soul ties, and we have the power to remove them too. We are already connected to everything, but we can strengthen this connection through creating soul ties via social or intimate interactions with them. Usually when we display some sense of vulnerability with another, whether it's a secret of ours or we connect physically, this is when a soul tie may be created. This causes us to feel a sense of closeness to them, but when we are trying to move away from them, it can also hinder us.

To remove a soul tie, picture the person you feel has a hold on you in your mind's eye, a couple of feet in front of you. Look down and see if in your mind's eye there are any cords connecting the two of you. They may look big or little, and stem from any part of your body. Remove the cord in your mind's eye with your dominant hand. When removing the cord, pull it out completely. Do not "cut" this cord as cutting the cord leaves the root of it within you.

Say to them aloud, "What's mine is mine, and what's yours is yours. I send your energy back to you with light and love and I call my energy back to me with light and love. You are fulfilled. I am fulfilled. You are free. I am free. I let you go, and I let myself move forward."

You can do this daily or as long as you feel you need to. You may have created multiple cords with them, especially if you spent much of your time and energy with them, so practicing this more than once is most likely helpful.

A Desirable Future

Whether you are going through a breakup, moving to a new city, or leaving your long-time job, the best way to move through change is to create a desirable future outcome you wish to move toward. Moving from first grade to second grade, to third grade and so on can be exciting, but at the end of each grade, we know there is just more school to come. All of it becomes a blur of tests, grades, and homework. The most exciting part about graduating from college is knowing you are officially done with all things school. The best way to move through change is to tell yourself that there is something extremely desirable on the other side. I mean, who wants to cross a bridge that has something negative on the other side of it? We want to cross bridges that lead to something better than where we are.

Think about your desired future.

(*What does your desired future look like?*

(*How do you feel in your desired future?*

(*What are you doing in your desired future?*

(*What's in your future that excites you?*

(*What have you always wanted that your desired future has?*

Positive Bitch Tip: When you can focus on this desired future, your undesirable past becomes boring, FAST. You won't want to think about the boring past when your desirable future is awaiting your arrival.

8

Positive Bitches Speak Life Over Their Life, Not Death

Taking Your Power Back from Your Words

Conscious Question:
"Are My Words Building or Breaking Me?"

Words Are Powerful

We've all been on the other side of someone's hurtful words and felt the sting that only words can provide. In that moment, we knew, words have power. We've also been on the other side of words that have made us feel on top of the world, like when our caregivers have said, "I'm so proud of you." We've been deeply moved by monologues in our favorite romantic movies, felt empowered by speeches, felt heard from poems, and gotten to experience other worlds through the words in books. Words have power, they have vibration, and they, for better or for worse, can affect us deeply.

**"The words of the reckless pierce like swords,
but the tongue of the wise brings healing."**

—Proverbs 12:18-19

Humans have the ability to communicate with others through our complex language systems, yet we use these systems to talk negatively about ourselves, spew hate on the internet, and cause harm to others. Words have power, but we are using this power to break ourselves and others down rather than using words to build ourselves and each other up. This is the biggest misuse of our power. If we knew how powerful our words were, we would cease to use them in such low-vibrational ways. The power of words is not a new concept, but I am here to remind you again of the fire that you play with.

**"The tongue has the power of life and death,
and those who love it will eat its fruit."**

—Proverbs 18:21

Positive Bitch Tip: There is a reason they call it *SPELL*-ing. When we are speaking about ourselves, regardless of whether it's positive or negative, we are speaking that circumstance into existence. We are casting spells when we speak. Every single word we say holds a vibration and affects us, as well as those around us. Your words are things, and they will take on a life of their own, especially if said enough times. The more you speak something, the more energy you are feeding that circumstance. If you are speaking positively over your life, you are speaking into existence positive circumstance. Whether or not you call it a "spell" doesn't matter. The energy of words will come to fruition.

If we are speaking negativity over ourselves, or others, we are practicing dark magic. We are using our power, but in a way that harms ourselves or another, this is what dark magic literally is. Speaking your worries, your problems, gossiping, and harping on what you do not like is a negative prayer. The more you focus on what you do not like in your life, the more you are casting the spell for that circumstance.

Positive Bitch Tip: Say what you wish to see. If you do not want to experience a certain circumstance, do not speak about that circumstance.

We cannot solve problems from the same vibration the problem was created from. If you keep speaking about the problem, you will attract more momentum in relation to it. The more you say, "I cannot do this," the more you will feel you cannot do what you are trying to accomplish.

> # Change your words to, "I am trying my best, and I can do whatever I put my mind to."

Focus on what you want to see in your reality and talk about that instead. Now, instead of casting negative prayers, you are casting positive ones. Instead of attracting more negativity, you are shifting your vibration higher to attract better vibrational solutions.

Your Words Are Your Wand That Creates Your World

If that explanation was too "woo-woo" for you, let's turn our attention to science...oh, and Confucius.

> **"The man who says he can, and the man who says he cannot, are both right."**
>
> **—Confucius**

Every word we speak, our subconscious mind hears. The more we tell our subconscious mind who we are, the more our subconscious mind believes it, and the more we wire in that trait. Our subconscious mind will not question what we say, regardless of how true it is. Every time we say, "I am _____," we are hypnotizing ourselves.

If we claim, "I am always broken up with," we will always be broken up with. If we claim, "I am naturally confident," we will be naturally confident. If we claim, "I cannot get over my ex," we will not be able to get over our ex. You are telling your mind and body how to operate, down to your cellular makeup, anytime you say "I." You are the one with the wand in hand, instructing your body how to think, feel and act, which then causes your outer reality to match that vibration.

> **Positive Bitch Tip:** Stop making jokes at your own expense, because you will have to pay up. Our subconscious mind doesn't know we are joking. So, even if you want to joke about how you're always single, DON'T. Think of all the colorful words in the world and pick literally anything else to say. You can claim to be excited about meeting new people, you can look forward to having your romantic life unfold for you, but you cannot and should not claim anything negative about yourself, even if it is a joke. If you want to joke, joke about how you are the hottest person in every room, the most successful at your firm, and how lavishly abundant you are. Now *that's* a positive prayer.

How to Take Your Power Back from Words

Our words are one of our most untapped and ignored tools, so it's time we revive this bitch. I know you would not walk into school, work, or a party with your makeup looking all dusty and crusty. So, I know that you will now also not walk into school, work, or a party with your words sounding all dusty and crusty. Pick your words like you pick your makeup, like you pick your shoes, like you pick anything that you physically show to the world. Your words are very much shown on you, even if it's in an unexplainable way. Your words are part of what makes up your vibration, and this is perceived by others. This means your words are just as important as your makeup or clothes are physically, so let's treat them that way.

Our Wounds Become Our Words and Our Words Become Our World

It's imperative that you become conscious of the language you are using about yourself. Use the questions below as journal prompts to become conscious of your inner world.

❤   *How do you react when you make a mistake?*

❤   *What do you call yourself when you don't get the answer right?*

❤   *What words do you use when you're having an inner dialogue?*

❤   *What words are writing your world?*

If you aren't sure about the words you use to refer to yourself, a good place to start is to think back on the words you were called growing up. What names did parents or peers use to refer to you?

Some names we may have been called growing up include but are not limited to:

✦ *Stupid*	✦ *Loser*
✦ *Ugly*	✦ *Weird*
✦ *Untalented*	✦ *Unpopular*
✦ *Annoying*	✦ *Freak*

If any of those words triggered you, good, they were meant to. We must not be afraid of words. We must get to know the worst of the words that were used against us so we can dismantle the pain associated with them. Many of us on a subconscious level are still calling ourselves the same name our parents and peers referred to us as. It's time to break this curse.

When you are repeatedly told you are not talented as a child, you give your power away by believing this lie. Once you believe someone else's word, you fall under their spell. Once under their spell, instead of living according to your own desires, you restrict yourself because you don't think you're good enough. Is this not a curse? To believe someone else's projected feelings about themselves and then limit your own life experiences?

These things are like familial curses. If your parents were always told they were stupid, they most likely gave their power away as children, believed this lie, and probably called you stupid too. If you were always called stupid, you also may have given your power away by believing this lie, and now you may call your own children stupid too. You must step out from under this veil of dark magic to reclaim the truth of your power and to see beyond the surface of these words.

We break familial curses when we stop repeating what was said to us, in our heads and to the next generation. Instead of calling ourselves stupid when we make a mistake, we must choose to see the lesson learned. Instead of calling the next generation stupid, we must choose to love our children with kind words.

> **Positive Bitch Tip:** A curse does not stop until you stop it.
> You have the chance to end a curse for your whole entire
> bloodline. You wouldn't be given this opportunity if you
> could not achieve lifting the veil. You can heal, and are
> already healing, yourself and the generations to come after.
> Be proud of the work you are doing.

204

Your Inner Child

Anytime I am about to call myself something that is mean, I imagine I am talking to my younger self, and that stops me in my tracks. If you wouldn't tell your five-year-old self whatever you're about to say to yourself now, don't say it at all, because that is who you are really talking to. When you are criticizing yourself, you're also criticizing your inner child.

I also apply this when I'm talking to others, especially with relatives, who I am more likely to say something harmful to. Before I let the words leave my mouth, I will visualize this relative as their innocent younger self. I remember that they too did not get all their needs met, they too have wounds, and they too are just trying to survive with what they know. While this isn't a magic bullet that will stop you from ever saying anything harmful, it does help.

Positive Word Reinforcement

In the same way you can hypnotize yourself, you can also hypnotize others by repeatedly telling them who they are. When we constantly tell our partner how bad a listener they are, they will continue to be a bad listener. Instead of telling them what they're doing wrong, highlight when they're doing something right with your words.

When they do listen, say, "I love how you listened so closely."

Focus and speak on what you like to attract more of it. Saying negative words about others is just as bad as saying them about yourself. What you give out you will get back, so think before you speak, let love leave your lips, and remember, once you say something, you cannot go back in time to take it back.

205

Reviving and Reprogramming

The words of others may have affected us, but we will not let them determine where we are going. Even if these words have hurt us in the past, we won't let them cause us to continuously suffer now. You can begin to reprogram yourself just by affirming positive attributes about yourself. You can say anything you wish to be true about yourself.

I am enough

I am successful

I am smart

I am confident

I am healthy

I am happy

I am whole

I am in tune with the Universe

I am naturally talented

I am courageous

I am lovable

I am strong

I am beautiful

Make sure that whatever follows your "I am" is something you want to be true about yourself. If what you are affirming about yourself isn't true at first, it doesn't mean it's not true at all. It means that it will be true in some time as you wire it in neurologically. You're not lying, you're just talking about who you are becoming. It can never be true if you do not start affirming it, so now is the time! It can feel silly at first to say these things when you don't believe them just yet, but the more you repeat these affirmations, the more you, and your subconscious mind, will believe them. Push through the moments when it feels uncomfortable. That is just your ego not liking the unfamiliarity of these words. The more you familiarize yourself, the easier it will be to claim these affirmations.

> **Positive Bitch Tip:** Affirmations don't work unless you work them. Saying one of these statements once will not do much. It's like watering a plant once and then never again. If you want to keep growing, you must keep watering yourself with positive statements. If you stopped watering a plant, it would die. If you stop watering this new version of you, it will die too. It's important to be consistent with affirmations because it will nourish your identity. These affirmations are planting the seeds of your new life. The more you practice them, the more you nourish them, the faster they will come into your reality.

You can say these affirmations aloud, or you can write them down. Both of these options have perks. I love to say my affirmations aloud while I am around my room. I have pasted note cards all around my mirror with positive statements so every time I look in the mirror, I remind myself to program in a positive affirmation instead of a negative one. I also pasted affirmations on the inside of my bathroom mirror so when I go to brush my teeth or wash my face, I am again prompted to do some affirmations. You can tape postcards or you can use your lipstick to write a positive statement on your mirror to remind yourself to practice your daily affirmations. We are busy people living busy lives, so it's easy for our affirmations to get away from us. To ensure you are watering yourself with affirmations, put them in places you often look so they can act as a reminder to build yourself up.

I also have a notebook in which I write out affirmations. I like writing out affirmations because it takes longer to write a sentence than it does to speak it. The longer I focus my attention on an affirmation, the more energy I am sending it, and the faster it is manifesting into my life. While we are writing, we make many more neurological connections than we would just speaking, which may prime you for moments of spiritual downloads or deeper awareness into your inner world. If you are going to write out your affirmations, I do suggest writing rather than typing, because typing takes away the time aspect that writing provides.

Mirror Work

Mirror work is saying affirmations while staring at yourself in the mirror. You may be thinking this sounds pointless, but I've had some of my most transformative moments just looking in the mirror and talking to myself.

After I experienced that initial spiritual download that I mentioned in the introduction, you know, the one where I realized I had to take my power back if anything was going to change, I felt looking in the mirror allowed me to get real with myself. Instead of being consumed by the external world, the mirror was a portal back to myself. It became a vehicle of self-connection. The true magic comes in when you switch your focus from your body to your own eyes.

In the past I used the mirror the wrong way—yes, there is a wrong way to use your mirror. We wrongly use our mirror when we use it to hate our God-given vessels! I spent so much of my time speaking negatively over my body, I missed the magic of my own being. As I practiced looking into my eyes while stating affirmations, I honestly felt bad for talking to myself the way I had been. I was given this body as a gift to experience being human, yet I was so mean to it. All my body has ever done is help me walk to beautiful places, see beautiful things, and...oh yeah, keep me ALIVE.

Instead of practicing self-hatred, I was practicing self-love. Instead of looking for what I thought was wrong with me, I started thanking God for everything that was right. As I continued with mirror work, the way I saw myself shifted. I was taken aback by my own beauty for the first time in my life. I didn't just see CiiCii, I saw myself from God's point of view. I saw a beautiful human. A magical multidimensional goddess with the power to create her dream life.

Looking into your eyes while affirming to yourself the truth of who you are allows for extreme transformation, because you are connecting with yourself visually and audibly. You're not looking at a tree while saying affirmations outside, or thinking about the color of your pen while writing affirmations down—you are looking at you, talking to you, connecting to you, and loving you.

Catch and Claim

While you are nourishing this new self, your old self will pop up here and there. Your old self may say, "I am not confident, and I cannot do this."

Positive Bitch Tip: Part of the evolution process is facing the older self while integrating the new self. This doesn't mean you are going backward; rather you are going deeper.

❤ *When you catch yourself saying a statement that isn't helpful to you, or you aren't sure whether it's helpful to you, ask yourself, "Are my words building me or breaking me?"*

If they are building you, you are good to go. If they are breaking you, take a pause. Take a breath. We don't want to claim projections from others or negative self-talk. That shit has nothing to do with us! Think about what words could nurture you back to a better feeling place, and claim that statement instead.

> **"I *claim* that I am working on my confidence and feeling better every day."**

This process is called Catch and Claim.

Catch and Claim: A process to interrupt negative self-talk and replace those words by claiming a new positive affirmation aloud.

The steps of this process are:

1. Have awareness of the negative self-talk from your past self coming up.

2. Ask yourself, "Are my words building me up or breaking me down?"

3. If they are building you up, you are done; however, if they are breaking you down, take a deep breath and go to next step.

4. Think of a positive affirmative statement to claim.

5. Say this aloud.

Spark Words

⸮ **Positive Bitch Tip:** Our world follows our words.

One of my personal favorite ways to use my words is to pick outlandish ones to get myself in a better mood and manifest with greater intensity. Our words affect how we feel. If I say, "I feel terrible," this will have a biochemical reaction in my body, and I will start to feel terrible. I choose specific sparkly words to heighten my mood and refocus. When someone asks me, "How are you?" I don't just say good—how boring. I say, "Fantastic, and life is getting better and better." When we use words that are not common to us, it can help interrupt a thought pattern or create a new one. Remember how I told you to pretend your ex is dead? "Dead" is a spark word too. It's so different, so shocking, that your brain hears you loud and clear. Ever see a dog tilt its head for a cookie? This is what I imagine the brain does when it hears a word we don't usually use.

Spark words vary from person to person because what is commonly used for one may not be commonly used for another. To find spark words, look up synonyms for positive words that you use to find a new fun way to use your power. Don't just say you're "fine," find words that sound more than just fine, and you'll start to feel that way too.

)
(**Positive Bitch Tip:** It's supposed to SPARK something, let it be shock-worthy and have FUN.

Cheat Sheet

Instead of:	Use:
I'm fine	I'm doing **fan-fucking-tastic**
I wonder what my ex is doing	My ex is **dead**
I'm feeling good	**Oh, damn I love** how good I'm feeling
I look alright	I am **a hot positive bitch** and I know it
I'm trying to do better	I **naturally improve** with each breath I take
I can't do this	I'm **literally fucking unstoppable**
I feel overwhelmed	**Boundaries are hot**, especially when I use them

9

Positive Bitches Believe Everything Happens for Opportunity

Taking Your Power Back from Contrast

*Conscious Question:
"What If This Is Happening
for Me?"*

The Why Behind Everything

You probably have heard the saying, "Everything happens for a reason."

Is this true? God only knows. No, seriously, I'm not sure. I've struggled for years with this concept, especially when my clients started letting me into their lives. When I had clients telling me their traumas, there was no way I could respond, "Well, everything happens for a reason." When I had a family friend who committed suicide, I again could not say, "Well, everything happens for a reason." I have seen tragedies happen across the globe and I cannot bring myself to utter those words because they do not feel, sound, or look right to me.

This doesn't mean I think things are random. It means I'm not sure how to fill in all the blanks. When I look back to connect the dots in my own life, I can see how even the most painful moments ultimately made me stronger or pushed me in a direction I am now thankful for. I don't know if things happen for a reason, but I do believe things happen *for* us. The thing is that the "for us" part is usually not immediately visible. When I was first writing this book, I was apprehensive in some ways because I have never written a book before. My job is to talk, and I am good at talking. You would think that writing is as easy as talking, but it was very different. I usually let my words flow through me, but having to write it down, having to look at every word, and wanting to perfect those words was a feeling I hadn't had before. After I got through the apprehension, and finally finished my first chapter, my computer glitched and deleted the whole entire first chapter. All five thousand words. I was devastated.

I thought, "Maybe I shouldn't even be writing a book," "Maybe this is a sign," and of course I asked the crowd favorite, "God, WHY?"

I tried for a full two days to revive the chapter. I spent hours on the phone and worked with a computer tech, but no one could salvage this chapter. I never had my computer glitch so when it deleted all my work, it struck me as very odd and upsetting. I gave myself a couple of days off to breathe and mourn my lost words. Over the course of these days, I started to have new thoughts, different thoughts, thoughts that weren't available to me when the chapter was first written. I started to receive words that I liked better than what I originally wrote. As I calmed down, gave myself space to breathe, I remembered that everything is energy. That original document was just energy. Energy can be transmuted, but it cannot be destroyed. My work may have been transmuted from this physical realm, but it still existed vibrationally.

Being a first-time author, chances are my first chapter wasn't *that* great anyway. I wasn't starting over; I was starting again, but this time with more information about what I wanted to write and how I wanted to structure it. I made myself some tea and sat down to begin again. When I finished rewriting the chapter, everyone who had read both versions, including me, agreed it was ten times better than the first "first chapter."

I realized the first version was wiped *for* me; it didn't happen *to* me.

There is an ancient Chinese proverb that is helpful when asking, "Do things happen for a reason?"

It goes something like this:

A very long time ago, a poor Chinese farmer lost his horse. All the neighbors came around and said, "Well, that's unlucky." The farmer simply said, "Maybe." Shortly after that, the horse returned and brought another horse back with him. All the neighbors then came around and said, "Well, isn't that lucky." The farmer simply said, "Maybe." The next day the farmer's son was trying to tame the new horse and fell, breaking his leg. All the neighbors came around and said, "Well, that's unlucky." The farmer simply said, "Maybe." A little while later, the emperor declared a war on the neighboring nation and ordered all able-bodied men to come fight. The farmer's son, being injured, was unable to fight. Many died or were badly injured during this war, but his son was spared. All the neighbors came around and said, "Well, isn't that lucky," to which the farmer replied, "Maybe," and so the story goes.

The moral of the story is that we do not know how one event can connect to or affect another. We may see an event as "bad" or "good," but we cannot tell how this will affect us in the long run. In life, things are more fluid than we think. Nothing is static. Everything affects everything. Instead of being attached to attaching meaning, we must remind ourselves that maybe we don't know why something is happening just yet, but we can trust ourselves and God, trust that we will somehow become stronger from it, and create opportunity where we can.

We have the power to determine how something is going to feel in our life based on the meaning we give it. Once something does happen, it's up to us to create meaning in a way that makes the circumstance not a source of suffering. I believe we can create our own meaning, possibility, and opportunity out of any circumstance, even when we don't want to, even when the circumstance is terrible. I believe that it's better to believe that things can and do happen for us, even if we do not immediately understand that. I believe tragedy can bear triumph if we take the shift in our life up on its potential opportunity.

Your Meaning Can Make You or Break You

Maybe it's the fighter in me, or the believer in me, but I'd rather spend my life believing that all is working for me than fearing it's not. What if I told you that you had the power to *decide* why things are happening? My beliefs about the world unfolding for me are my beliefs out of *choice*. If you want to start putting a positive spin on even the worst of circumstances, you must *choose* to believe that in some way, somehow, this event is unfolding for you. You may not be able to understand how or why it's happening for you, but must decide to trust it anyway. Think about all the times you thought your life was going one way, but then It took a detour in a completely opposite, positive direction. The truth is, we don't know everything, so why not trust in positive possibilities?

> **Positive Bitch Tip:** Your strength and happiness are one faith-based decision away.

Becoming Lost to Be Found Again

Even feeling "lost" serves a purpose. One day when I was questioning whether I was on the right path, I turned off the distractions of the 3D world and traveled inward to connect with myself and God, and this is what I heard:

*You're not lost; you're just ready for the next big thing,
and there's a difference.*

You're not lost; your soul is just evolving.

You're not lost; your vibration is changing and wanting differently.

You're not lost; you're growing.

You're not lost; you're discovering new parts of yourself.

*You're not lost; you're realizing the "old" is no longer in vibrational
alignment with you.*

You're not lost; but being found right now.

Feeling lost is our ego's way of trying to label what our soul is actually going through energetically. Don't see this feeling as a sign to stop, but to keep moving. You wouldn't stop driving halfway to your destination, so don't stop growing halfway to where you wish to be. Lean into the realization that feeling "lost" is not what you thought it was. You're not in the wrong, you're just ready for more!

Leaning into Loneliness to Become a Lioness

Feeling lonely gets a bad rap, especially because most of us misread what loneliness is trying to convey to us. Feeling lonely has nothing to do with being alone. I'm sure you've experienced being in a crowded room but feeling completely alone, and then had times when you were alone physically but felt fulfilled anyway.

> **Positive Bitch Tip:** Feeling lonely isn't about your connection to others as much as it is about your connection to yourself. When feeling lonely, what you're actually seeking is connection to self and Source Energy (God).

When I met with a shaman, I asked her why people experience loneliness. She explained to me that, because we go from being connected to everything, and having a knowingness that we are one with all, to a fragment of our soul getting stuffed into human vessels, we forget how deeply and divinely plugged in we truly are. We lose that knowingness of the Law of One. I see loneliness as humanity's original wound. We agree to be human, and part of that experience is agreeing to forget our true connective nature.

If you want to feel your natural connection to all, grounding practices are extremely helpful. Grounding practices include:

+ *Prayer*
+ *Generalized talking to God or your angels*
+ *Meditation*

+ *Earthing (walking barefoot on earth)*
+ *Sungazing*
+ *Spending time in nature*
+ *Journaling*

I went through many seasons of feeling lonely as I was healing my codependent habits. It was extremely hard at times, but I knew there had to be something I could gain from the emotional experience. In that time, I created a new habit I call dating the Divine.

Dating the Divine: A process to ground yourself in times of loneliness or chaos by connecting to God, your spirit guides, yourself, and/or nature.

219

I would often go to a local harbor, bringing a blanket, my notebook to journal in, and my phone to listen to a meditation. Whether I was feeling lonely or chaotic, I brought all my problems and took it straight up to God. I would journal out my worries, talk to God, and cuddle up to the calming frequencies of the earth. Instead of running away from my loneliness, I gave myself space to feel it instead. The more I allowed myself to feel, the faster the feeling left my body. During my dates with the Divine, I channeled wisdom that shocked me, released what felt like one hundred pounds of emotion, and learned a plethora of things about myself. I always left that harbor feeling better than when I got there.

> **Positive Bitch Tip:** Talking to God is cheaper than a therapist, and you don't have to pay to be in nature. Use these free healing tools to your advantage.

One of the reasons I started dating the Divine is that I really didn't have friends at that time. With no boyfriend and not many friends, I had myself and God to talk to. Since God seemed to be the only one answering me, I kept going back to Him for more.

> **Positive Bitch Tip:** Sometimes we have to lose the wrong people to let in the right ones. Don't take it personally, take it vibrationally.

Obviously, God isn't an actual person, but because I had so much alone time, I got extremely close to the divine. I could have easily assumed there was something wrong with me that I lost all my friends and a relationship, but instead of taking it personally, I took it vibrationally. This was a season that was going to hold my biggest transformation yet, why try to fight it? I needed this alone time to peel back the layers of my ego and go back home to my true authentic frequency. I stopped feeling lonely and began to feel like a lioness claiming her inherent power.

Your Body Has a Message

Feeling disconnected to our body is a feeling many of us face. Most of our souls have incarnated many times in different bodies. While we do not consciously remember this, our soul does, which can contribute to us feeling uncomfortable in our own skin. To make matters worse we are inundated with images of what "perfect" looks like, and if we don't look exactly the same as those images, we may feel insecure. We get stuck in loops of comparing ourselves to others and never feeling pretty enough, skinny enough, curvy enough, and so on. This cycle of insecurity quickly turns into us hating our own bodies.

I struggled with my body image for many years as most young girls do. I couldn't figure out why I incarnated in the body I had as I had so much hatred for it. I thought my body was faulty and it felt like it was working against me as my thyroid wasn't operating properly. I asked my spirit guides, "Why do I have this body?" What they showed me brought clarity and peace. While in deep meditation my guides walked me into what looked like a huge department store. However, instead of their being different clothing on the racks, different designers, and name brands, there were all different bodies. Not in a gory way, but in a way that said, "Choose your body like you choose your jeans!" There were bigger bodies, skinny bodies, medium bodies, and strong bodies, all hanging on hangers. Any body type you can imagine was there! All the bodies were shown in adult form and ranged in skin tone.

Each body had a tag just like a pair of jeans at a store would have an attached price tag. On each of the tags, instead of the name brand, price and barcode being listed it listed the possible illnesses this body may develop, the positives of embodying this body, the weaknesses and the strengths of the body. I was confused how one body could have so many different possible outcomes of health or illness. They explained to me this was because of free will. What we decide while on planet Earth will dictate if we lean into the possible illnesses or strengths. Depending on how you treat your body and depending on what circumstances may unfold will depend on the outcome you get. The biggest part of the tag was the lesson you could receive from embodying this body. My guides in this moment expressed to me that each body had encoded with it many different opportunities of learning. My guides showed me that before we incarnate on planet Earth, our soul chooses the body it's going to learn the most from.

Here I was complaining about my body when I was the one who chose it. Instead of learning how to work with my body, anytime it didn't look exactly how I wanted, or wasn't operating perfectly, I decided to hate it. This only actively works against our body as it creates stress hormones which cause further harm. Rather than trying to run from my body, I knew it was time to find a way to work with it. In this moment my feelings of "Why was I given this body," turned into, "I'm grateful for this body because it is one of my greatest teachers helping my soul evolve." I felt guilty for hating the body I chose and ignoring the messages it was trying to convey through illness and physical feelings of pain.

222

Our body is always talking to us but that doesn't mean we're always listening. Our body sends us signals daily. When we need rest it will cause us to feel tired so we take a nap. When we're holding onto too much energy, it will cause us to feel anxious so we find a way to release the extra energy. When we're holding onto negativity, our body will cause us to feel pain so we can transmute the energetic imbalance. Our body is always working for us. When we're awake, when we're asleep, when we're happy and when we're stressed.

It's always trying to bring us back to homeostasis.

Our body is always helping us, but are we always helping our body?

I didn't choose my body based on how sexually attractive I would be to others, but because my soul wanted to learn from it. Focusing on what's wrong with our body physically only causes us to grow hatred for it. Focusing on how you can help your body instead of just focusing on what your body looks like can help you reconnect with it. This will help you switch your perception from how other people view you to how you feel.

The following journal prompts can help you connect with your body:

☾ *What would make my body feel healthy?*

☾ *What would make my body feel energized?*

☾ *What does my body need from me right now to heal?*

☾ *What does my body need more of?*

☾ *What does my body need less of?*

Your body isn't your enemy, it's your support system. Our body is how we are able to have this earthly experience. Our bodies are not all meant to look the same. We chose different bodies, different lessons, and different experiences for our own soul reasons. There is no point in comparing ourselves to another because we were never meant to look like them in the first place. Their lessons have nothing to do with ours!

Our bodies' possible obstacles are also our bodies' opportunities to learn. We may need to learn balance, compassion, self-love, discipline, self-acceptance, or something else. What do you think your body is trying to teach you?

How to Take Your Power Back from Contrast

We can use the circumstances in our life to create momentum to move us forward. Painful and perceived negative experiences are spiritual invitations to level up. While our physical self may be going through hardship, our spiritual self, on a higher plane, is gaining lessons learned, strength, and understanding. Remember, not all our soul can manifest on earth at once. Our soul is always in many different planes. Even if our physical self doesn't understand at this moment, it doesn't mean our soul isn't having positive progress.

How can we help our physical self out? We may not be able to control everything, but we can control what meaning we give situations, which will also control how we feel about it. If you want to survive in a way that doesn't feel terrible, your job is to find the silver lining in every situation.

From Why to What

When something happens that feels bad, you may jump to saying, "Why me?" Interrupt this.

Instead of asking "Why," ask "What."

(*What can I do to make myself feel better?*

(*What meaning can I create out of this situation to empower me?*

(*What can I do to shift my emotions?*

(*What can I learn from this situation?*

(*What opportunity does this circumstance allow me to have now?*

"What" will lead you to actionable steps you can take to feel better, while "why" leaves you in a hamster wheel of misery. Asking yourself "what" will help you shift your mindset, focus, and energy, therefore elevating your emotions. It can also invite in higher-vibrational thoughts that have the potential to lead you to your purpose and other passions. When I went through my breakup, I decided to start asking "what" instead of "why," and it led me to creating my desired life.

Use this circumstance to create the momentum you need to birth a new cycle.

) **Positive Bitch Tip:** The most important "what" question is, "What if everything is working out for me?"

The reason this holds such power is because it flips us into a state of faith and can anchor us into a higher vibration. When we assume all

225

is working out for us, it does. When we assume the best, it happens. When we assume that everything will ultimately unfold in a way that helps us, it unfolds in exactly that way. When you're assuming in a positive direction, it allows you to attract more positive experiences. Don't let one moment ruin your whole point of attraction.

Everything can mean nothing, or everything can mean something. I choose to live in meaning and purpose. If you don't know the meaning of why something is happening, or you're not sure what you want it to mean yet, at least don't create a negative meaning around it. Being in the unknown is better than telling ourselves everything is going wrong. When you create positive meaning around circumstances, you take your power back from them.

> **Positive Bitch Tip:** You haven't been knocked down a million times, but have found a million ways to stand back up.

You haven't been broken a million times,
but have found a million ways to rebuild yourself.

You haven't been hurt a million times,
but have found a million ways to feel pleasure again.

You haven't been rejected a million times,
but redirected a million different ways.

You haven't failed a million times,
but found a million ways that don't work.

There is always a positive meaning if you create it for yourself.
Everything is an opportunity if you allow it to be.

New Optical Prescription

Over dinner one night, I had a deep conversation with my grandma about my uncle, who has a brain injury. At just seventeen years old, my uncle was in a car accident that changed him forever, as well as everyone who loved him. He was sitting on the hood of a still car, hanging out with his friends. Suddenly one of his friends thought it would be funny to hit the gas pedal full force and then slam on the brakes while my uncle was still on the hood. When his friend hit the brake, my uncle flew off the car and hit his head on concrete.

His last words were him pleading, "Ambulance, ambulance."

The ambulance was immediately called. His health and consciousness were rapidly declining. When he was admitted to the hospital, all the doctors told my grandma there was no chance he was walking out of there alive. My grandma, grandpa, parents, aunts, uncles, priests, and other prayer warriors assembled around my injured uncle and went into prayer mode, decreeing life over his injured body. The doctors recounted that they had never had so much prayer in the hospital. My uncle is still alive and now forty-two years old. He is currently six foot four, about two hundred and seventy pounds, in diapers, understands some things but cannot speak, and cannot walk because half of his body is paralyzed. My grandparents have never given up on my uncle, and prayer surrounds him to this day.

During this conversation, my grandma was asking, "Why would this happen?" and it hit me, another spiritual download.

In that moment I understood, like I know my own name, that my grandma as her human self would most likely never understand why this happened, and that was okay. Her purpose wasn't to *understand* this, it was to *experience* it. She, as her human self, didn't need to understand the circumstances for her soul to absorb what was expanding within her. Not only is her soul evolving from this lifetime by learning through hardship, but she is the reason my uncle is able to learn so much in one lifetime. Her higher self agreeing to be his mother in this life is what afforded him the possibility to go through rapid soul evolution. As my uncle is teaching my grandma, my grandma is teaching my uncle. Their souls have helped one another transform and evolve through many lifetimes, which is evident through their deep connection and my grandma's unconditional love.

My grandma, my uncle, and his accident are not random. This sounds illogical to our human ears. It is illogical when you just look at this physical plane of existence. Our greater plan isn't shown to our human self, but made by our higher self in conjunction with God. It wasn't easy to say these words to her, or anyone else, because it doesn't make "earth-like" sense, but there is more than this earth! I didn't say this to give her hope that there is meaning in this experience. I said this to her because, although I don't know it all, I *know* she is fulfilling some plan in her higher self's eyes.

228

My place isn't to proclaim what my grandma's lessons are, but if I had to use my intuition to understand this circumstance through her higher self, I would say her biggest lesson has to do with learning how to balance giving and receiving love. She gives out so much energy and love, not only to my uncle, but to anyone in need. When my grandma, as a much younger woman, only had one dollar left in her bag, she gave that last dollar away to the collection at church. I know most people think their grandma is a saint, but I'm pretty sure mine literally is. When she got back in the car, she noticed there was something under her foot. When she looked down, she saw it was a five-dollar bill. She needed that money to put food on the table, and somehow, it was provided. In this instance, when she gave up her last dollar, she was also able to receive when she found the five-dollar bill under her foot. This was an obvious physical exchange. However, sometimes, we are so used to giving, we forget how to receive. We get stuck in a cycle of giving out, and we end up feeling depleted all the time.

We are born instinctively knowing how to breathe with perfect balance. We exhale, we inhale, we exhale, we inhale, you know how this goes. If we only exhaled, we would deplete ourselves of carbon dioxide. If we only inhaled, we would overdose on oxygen. Breathing, for the most part, is something we just know how to do, and we are pretty good at keeping the balance throughout our lives. We, however, are not born instinctively knowing how much to give and get. This is mostly learned. If we only give or only get, we will not be able to achieve balance, and will therefore feel either depleted, or totally self-consumed.

I believe my grandma's soul is learning how to receive goodness, help from others, and grounding so she may feel safe in this earth plane. I believe one of her soul purposes is to teach unconditional love by being a living example. She has deeply affected all thirty and counting grandchildren because we see how she takes care of my uncle day in and day out, and we are all better for it. We understand that, regardless of capability or disability, every human comes with value and purpose. In a world that makes you feel so replaceable, my grandma has shown us that is not the case when she's around. No matter what mistakes we make, wrong turns we may take, she will always be there to love us and help us.

There are some things our human self will never understand because our human emotional self didn't choose that circumstance—our higher spiritual self did, as it is trying to grow during this incarnation. We didn't choose that sibling or that terrible boss; our higher self

229

did, so that we may evolve. Our higher self chooses many of the difficult events that unfold in our life. To our eternal higher self, this event isn't a big deal. It happens in the blink of an eye. To our human self, it may be very traumatic. If you cannot understand an event, person, or situation in your life, there is no promise that your human self will, and you don't need to force yourself to either. Expand your view from your human eyes to your spiritual ones.

> **Positive Bitch Tip:** Anytime something unfolds that I find difficult, I immediately switch my prescription from my "human eyes" to my "higher self eyes." This allows me to see my current circumstance from a higher perspective. We can either create meanings from our higher self that are going to elevate us, empower us, and help us move forward, or we can create meanings from our human self that depress us, disempower us, and make us stagnant.

I had to switch my prescription to my higher self when I was struggling with dermatitis, a recurring bumpy rash on my face. My human way of seeing this situation was wonky. It made me feel frustrated, powerless, embarrassed, and I honestly felt ugly. I was very uncomfortable in my own skin. I hated waking up every day and seeing a rash on my face and felt completely lost on how to solve the problem. At the time, my body started to fall apart further. I stopped getting my period, I had no energy, and my mood was all over the place. I felt worse than terrible. I lost interest in most things, and was forcing myself through my life day in and day out.

To level up my optical prescription, I had to put on my higher self's eyes. While I couldn't find the cause behind the dermatitis, I started to wonder if maybe dermatitis was going to take me further than my spiritual awakening ever could. I went to a naturopathic doctor and found out I had sensitivities to many of the foods I was eating daily, and my gut health was all over the place. I was eating foods that my body didn't agree with and drinking too much caffeine. I would have never gone to a naturopathic doctor to further check in on my health if it weren't for dermatitis. I started to see how it was causing me to shift my somewhat healthy lifestyle to a *very* clean lifestyle. I've been wanting to be a clear vessel to upgrade my spiritual abilities, but that couldn't happen when I was cluttering and polluting my own body. Dermatitis caused me to change my diet, my detergent, and my toothpaste, create a more natural routine, reduce my caffeine consumption, and alter how I moved my body. Ultimately, dermatitis was teaching me to take better care of my hormones and my body. It is still leading me to balance and detox. I had treated the symptoms of my problems for so long, dermatitis created momentum for me to take it further and finally pushed me to treat the actual root of all my health issues.

Now I am healing my thyroid, liver, and overall hormones.

When your human eyes aren't working, try to view the situation from your higher self's eyes.

♥   ***Ask yourself, "What would my higher self/soul say to me in this situation?"***

You can journal or meditate on this question. Be open to what may come through. Even if you don't understand it now, have faith that it will all come together. Why? Fretting will never take you to the places that faith can uplift you to.

10

Positive Bitches Have Faith

Standing in Your Power

Conscious Question:
"Do I Have Faith in the
Positive or in the Negative?"

Got Faith?

Faith means you trust in something that is unseen, unheard, or unrealized. We've all "got faith." However, what we have faith in varies. Some of us have faith that only bad things will happen to us, that nothing ever goes right, and that we lose more than we win. Others have faith that only good things unfold for them, everything is always going according to schedule, and they can only win or gain information to level up.

> **Positive Bitch Tip:** Whether we have faith in the good or the bad, we are having faith. You don't necessarily need to develop faith because you already have faith in something, but you may need to shift what you are focusing on and trusting in.

What we practice having faith in, we will get good at having faith in. If I practice having faith that negative things will happen, not only am I attuning myself to a frequency I do not wish to experience, but I'm on the lookout for negativity, because it's already in my mind. If you want to shift your point of attraction, try switching your prescription from your human eyes to your soul's or higher self's eyes. This will help you understand that your current point of view isn't all there is, and all is unfolding according to plan. The more you interrupt seeing your circumstances from your human eyes, and switch to seeing your circumstances from your soul's eyes, the more curiosity and positive faith will come about.

233

> **Positive Bitch Tip:** Your journey may take longer, it may be harder, but you will always end up with the exact people, places, opportunities, and tools that are necessary for your growth and expansion when you have faith in yourself.

God would not grant us a desire, and then deplete us of any and all resources needed to make that desire physically manifest. You're in the process. Keep going.

You Are a Cofounder

Much of our doubt in the positive comes from our ego, due to its limited perception.

Thinking from your ego may sound like:

+ *I am all alone.*
+ *There is not enough room for everyone's success.*
+ *Other people are just luckier than me.*

+ *I don't have the resources to do what I want.*
+ *I can't be successful.*

If you're thinking like this, you are forgetting that you are a cofounder of your life. You're forgetting that you don't have to do everything alone, and there are shifts happening that you may not be able to see. The other cofounder, that's God. There are certain tasks that you must do as cofounder, and other tasks that are best done when given to your *other* cofounder. Essentially, you and God are in business, baby! Your job is to know what you want in your mind and feel as if it's already yours. If you want a new job, see yourself in your mind's eye at this new job, and feel the gratitude of waking up and doing something you love every day. Plug into this frequency as much as you can.

> ## Each day, say, "I am so happy and grateful now that I _____ because it makes me feel _____,"

Put on music that makes you feel good, envision your desires in your mind's eye, and feel as if it's happening right in this moment. The more we attune ourselves to the frequency we want, the more we pull it toward us. Not only does this help with manifestation, but it feels good to feel good now!

How this job will align is not your job to work out; that's on God. You don't need to run around, stressed-out, begging people to hire you. You need to know what you want, see it and feel it, and your cofounder will align you with the right people at the right time in the right space. As soon as we start thinking about the how, we knock ourselves out of vibration. We may think about the job we want, which makes us feel good, but then start thinking about the how and immediately feel worse, which causes our frequency to drop. Do not worry about the how. Don't think about the how. Don't get stressed about the how. If anything, be curious and in awe of how God moves energy around so the Universe can give you exactly what you want. Get excited that you don't have to do everything on your own. Feel empowered that you have an amazing cofounder to help you achieve all that you desire.

Feeling in awe, excited, and empowered is what allows you to receive your manifestation. Feelings of doubt shut you off like a light switch blocking your reception to the high-vibe things you desire.

If I ever slip into having faith in fear rather than faith in myself, I immediately remind myself that all is unfolding for me, even if I cannot see it. I'll say a little something like this:

I know it is all coming together for me. I don't know how everything will unfold, but I don't need to know how, so thank you God. It will work out in ways I can't even anticipate, so thank you God. Even if what I want isn't in my direct point of view, it's in God's, and it's happening for me. God is placing the right people in the right place at the right time for me and delivering it to me through the Universe. I am always provided for. The Universe is forever shifting in my energetic favor and bringing to me all that I want. This is exciting! I'm so curious how it will all unfold, and I'm only feeling better and better with each day that passes by.

Your Backup

Our physical mind cannot see what our spiritual mind...and spiritual team...can.

You're not alone while you're here on earth; even when it looks like no one is physically supporting you, you have your cofounder, and did I mention, a whole entire team assisting you along your way. Remember how I mentioned spirit guides? It's about time we get a little esoteric up in here! If you think I've already blown past being esoteric, then it's about to get *very* esoteric up in here.

I don't want you to blindly believe anything I say. I want you to bring a healthy dose of skepticism and try this out for yourself. Your soul will lead you to new doors, but you must start knocking on those doors to be let in. I invite you to be curious about what I say, but ultimately always listen to your own voice.

We all have an assigned guardian angel we can call on at any time. Every single one of us has a different guardian angel that is ours and only ours. Archangels are different. Archangels, such as Archangel Michael, move around to many different souls, but can also be called on by us at any time. Archangels are so expansive, and because energy is nonlocal, they can assist fifty different people at the same time. Just as some of our soul's energy is in our body, and other parts of our soul also exist in other realms, archangels can lend their energy to many different people in different places. There are also ascended masters, who are highly evolved souls who had lives on earth, like Jesus, the Blessed Mother, and the Buddha. These spirit guides are ready to assist when we call on them. There are even loving ancestors and pets you can call on when you need guidance, support, or comfort.

I call this group of beings my "spirit team." We all have a spirit team, made up of beings that will help us based on our unique life journey. If your journey includes you being a scientist, you may have some spirits as part of your team that were also scientists in their day, and are now still working in that field, just on the other side. If you are a musician, you most likely wouldn't have spirits who were involved in science while here on earth, but spirits who were musicians instead. If you've always been drawn to a certain archangel or ascended master, that energy is most likely part of your team. If you feel a loved one's presence—perhaps your grandma, for example—they are also most likely part of your team.

If you want to call out to your spirit team, you can say, "Highest healing and loving spirit guide, connect to me now. Thank you."

Then ask your spirit guide to show that they are there. You can ask them to show you a sign.

"Spirit guide of highest healing and love, show me a sign of _____ to confirm you are here."

This sign may come in the next hour or the next week. You

can also ask them to activate a sensation immediately within your body for a faster confirmation.

"Spirit guide of highest healing and love, activate a sensation in my hands. Thank you."

Once you feel that, ask them to elevate the feeling.

"Elevate the sensation. Thank you."

This process is something I regularly tell my clients to do. One of my clients—let's call her Chelsea—called on her guides to create a sensation in her feet when she was bored while getting her hair done. Chelsea felt the sensation right away, but because she is a hypnotist herself, and knows how to move her energy, she didn't believe her guides were responsible for what she felt.

She said to them, "Okay, maybe that was you, but I want to feel a sensation, this time in my hands, so blatant, so obvious, that I know it's not me, but you."

Her hair stylist began talking to her, and she stopped thinking about the sensation in her feet. They ended up chit-chatting for some time as she got her hair washed in the sink. When the hair stylist began blowing Chelsea's hair out, Chelsea suddenly felt extreme pressure in her hands.

She started screaming, "Oh my God, oh my God, my hands are cramping."

The hair stylist said, "That happens to me all the time, because I'm always holding the blow dryer."

Chelsea said, "Oh! I must have somehow picked up your energy, because I've never in my life felt this sort of sensation before."

The hair stylist's assistant interrupted and began talking to the hair stylist. Chelsea just sat looking at herself in the mirror. Her mind was still. It wasn't until she had a moment of quiet that she was flooded with the knowingness that the sensation she'd just had was indeed her spirit guides. She didn't believe the first sensation her guides sent her, so they sent her exactly what she asked for, a more intense version! Your guides will give you exactly what you ask for, so be clear and trust that it's them. The more you practice making contact, the easier it will be, and the more belief you will have in them.

You can also ask direct questions. Highest healing guides will not give you information you are not ready to know. If you are meant to learn a lesson or develop a strength, your spirit guide will lovingly guide you in another direction. Spirit guides do not lie. If they are speaking anything that is negative, that is not a spirit guide but another energetic entity. There are many entities out there, just as there are many different people. The reason we say "highest healing and loving spirit guide" is so we specifically call on the energy we

239

wish to connect with. Do not call on just any entity. Only call on those from God's white light.

If you ever get uncomfortable, say, "Any energy not walking in the white light of God, I command you to leave now."

You can also use white sage or palo santo to cleanse your space. I cleanse my room daily. Be sure to open a window or a door to let the lower-vibrational energy out. If you're cleansing your space, that original energy needs to go somewhere. I walk around my room with sage or palo santo and I say, "Only the highest-vibrational energy is allowed in this space."

Not Giving Your Power Away to Other Sources

It's almost as if we try to give away our power sometimes. We are so quick to trust a psychic, horoscopes, tarot cards, even a TikTok prediction of what our life is going to look like. As soon as we hear a negative possible outcome, we lose it. I used to have some horoscope apps on my phone, but every time I looked at them, they got more negative. I decided that no app or other person was going to tell me how I was going to live my life. My life is for me to decide.

It's not that there aren't very talented psychics in the world; there are. There are people who are tapped in, have a gift, and want to share. They aren't the problem. One problem I see is that, while there are gifted souls with pure intentions, there are also people who are just out for money. They will purposely give you a negative reading so that you need more information, have to book another session, and eventually become reliant on them. Another problem is that life isn't predestined. While a psychic may be able to see one outcome, this doesn't mean it will be *the* outcome you experience. There are unlimited potential outcomes that exist. When you set your attention on one of those possible outcomes, you begin to set into motion that potential. The more energy you put toward that potential, the more it will grow and eventually solidify into the 3D. A psychic may not be lying, but they aren't telling the whole truth either. The whole truth would be that what they're telling you is one possible outcome of *unlimited* possibilities.

When it comes to horoscopes, we usually don't even know who is writing the information. I saw an interview with a woman who was the CEO of a popular horoscope app. She literally said that her company would purposely write negative potentials to put people into a fear state so that the audience would keep checking back on the app. No matter the industry, there will be corrupt people, and companies, within it just trying to make money. That CEO wanted more usage which would drive up her numbers, but she wasn't giving accurate information.

Psychics and horoscopes sometimes end up limiting us. I have had clients tell me that they will not date someone because of their horoscope. This never made sense to me. When people say, "What's your sign?" they are asking for your sun sign. They take this one piece of information and then make a whole entire decision off it. The issue here is that we are not just our sun sign. Our sun sign influences our energy, but it is not who we are. If you have ever seen an astrological chart, you know that we are made up of many different energies; as a society, we have just zeroed in on the sun sign. As a Capricorn, I "best" get along with Virgos and Taurus, according to astrology. It happens that my mom is a Virgo, and my sister is a Taurus. Sure, we get along well, but we also fight like cats and dogs. My boyfriend is an Aries, and that supposedly does not get along well with Capricorns, yet we have been together now for seven years. If I were to shut him out when we met just because of his sign, I would have lost out on this beautiful journey we are on. You don't know what lessons are in store for you. Maybe you actually need someone with a sign that you're not fond of because it's going to help you expand, grow, and learn. The point is, one sign doesn't make up a whole entire person, and when you give your power away to a sign, you strip yourself of experiences.

> **Positive Bitch Tip:** Someone's sun sign is good data to keep on the back burner, but it's not good enough data to make decisions with.

I've even seen people experience extreme emotional upset because Mercury was going into retrograde, and society has decided that means something "bad." By the way, don't let planets take your power away either. All that Mercury retrograde means is that Mercury looks like it's moving backward, even though it really isn't. People have taken this to mean that when a planet is in retrograde, it will also mean their lives will go backward too. Retrogrades are a time of reflection, revisiting, and reexamining. Yes, the energy of Mercury may be shifting, but that doesn't mean it's going to affect us in a negative way. I've found that, every time Mercury was in retrograde, my life leveled up in amazing ways. Sometimes it was uncomfortable, but it was always for my highest good in the end. It allowed for transformation and growth, exactly what I came here to Planet Earth for!

> **Positive Bitch Tip:** The energy on the planet may shift, but it's just energy, it's not a dictator. Energy cannot force things to happen, it can only influence. You are still the driving force in your life, so act like it!

Standing in Your Power

We are the magnets drawing everything into our life. As Positive Bitches, we use our external to help us understand our internal.

Remember, we may have some energy attached to our auric field we are unaware of, energy from possible past lives and our childhood that we are unconscious of. Only about 5 percent of the day are we conscious of ourselves and our life. Give yourself some grace, and then give yourself some more grace. You may have aligned with negative experiences in your past, but this is not your fault.

> **Positive Bitch Tip:** Just because you've aligned with such circumstances in your past, that has nothing to do with your present or your future. Lay down your past and let it rest in peace. If you got yourself here, you can get yourself anywhere.

We manifest experiences based on our dominant thoughts and emotions that make up our energetic signature. Our emotions, however, are the most magnetic force, stronger than our minds. Therefore, it is our emotions that mostly take over when manifesting. When you keep manifesting experiences that you do not like, it's not because you necessarily *thought* about that specific event, it's more because you felt a similar way with a different circumstance.

Let's say a minor car accident would cause you to feel annoyed. If this circumstance were to actually happen, it doesn't mean you thought about a minor car accident; it means you've already been feeling annoyed, so annoyed that it started to become a dominant feeling, and you now just manifested another experience to feel even more annoyed in. Your emotions are attracting similar feeling circumstances to retrigger the same emotion, giving you more of what you're already feeling.

> **Positive Bitch Tip:** The Universe assumes that whatever you're feeling, you're wanting more of.

> # To find the root emotion that is attracting your experiences, ask yourself, "What am I feeling right now?"

That emotion is the culprit. That emotion is what is drawing these experiences to you. We often manifest different circumstances with the same emotional outcome because we are not becoming curious enough to change our point of attraction. Most of the emotional experiences we attract are mirrors of our childhood. Many of us are subconsciously emotionally addicted to the experience we had in childhood. If our childhood was very up and down, we probably experience life now as very up and then down. If our childhood was mostly happy, we may be mostly happy. Keep this in mind when analyzing the emotional outcome you are experiencing.

You Are Your Own Best Psychic

Positive Bitch Tip: The best psychic for you is...YOU. Your life is constantly shifting, based on your energetic signature. This means that, as you shift your thoughts and feelings, you shift your energetic signature, which means you shift your life. If you want to know what your future will look like, look at your current thoughts, beliefs, actions, habits, and behaviors.

Your point of power is in the present, because you can change your present at any moment. If you don't like your life, don't get mad; get everything you want by using your current external reflection to fine-tune your internal point of attraction.

> **"Watch your thoughts; they become words.**
> **Watch your words; they become actions.**
> **Watch your actions; they become habits.**
> **Watch your habits; they become character.**
> **Watch your character; it becomes your destiny."**

> **—Lao Tzu**

245

Anchoring in Your Most Positive Bitch Self

Your future desired self already exists, just as your past self exists too. Whichever version you tap into most of the time in the present moment will dictate who you get to be. To shift your point of attraction, you must connect with HER, your future self. She knows what you really want, she knows how you got it, she holds the blueprint for your dream life. To connect to your future self, think about your desired life, desired health, desired thoughts, desired mindset, desired body, desired career, desired partner, desired family life, desired lifestyle, desired home, desired neighborhood, desired friendships, and so on.

What you are seeing as you desire this is your most Positive Bitch self, living their most Positive Bitch life, embodying Positive Bitchitude. She is HER.

How do we get there from here?

By deciding who we are as a Positive Bitch and showing up as her every single day to anchor in that point of attraction. We get good at what we practice. To anchor in this vibration, we must practice it. This will allow you to tap into a higher timeline, rather than being constricted by who you think you are.

"The good news is that the moment you decide that what you know is more important than what you have been taught to believe, you will have shifted gears in your quest for abundance. Success comes from within, not without."

—Ralph Waldo Emerson

246

Success comes from within, and it comes a lot faster when we have our ego lined up with our vision.

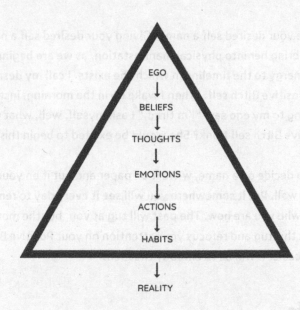

EGO
↓
BELIEFS
↓
THOUGHTS
↓
EMOTIONS
↓
ACTIONS
↓
HABITS
↓
REALITY

To create HER, we want to go straight to the root of our ego and work from there. If everything stems from our ego, that's where we will want to start. Instead of wasting our time trying to change the external, but then feeling uncomfortable and going back to what feels familiar, starting with the ego allows for a more seamless shift. This is how you actually change your self-concept, or how you see yourself.

The Ego

If you don't like what you look like, or what your life looks like, it's because you're listening to an outdated ego. Instead of listening to the faulty programming of your past ego, let's start listening to your desired self. Your ego self will try to pull you back into the comfort of what you know, but the more you refocus on your desired self, the closer you pull her toward you.

Let's give your desired self a name. Giving your desired self a name starts to bring her into physical manifestation, as we are beginning to feed energy to the timeline in which she exists. I call my desired self my Positive Bitch self. When I wake up in the morning, instead of listening to my ego say, "I'm tired," I ask myself, well, what would my Positive Bitch self think? She would be excited to begin this day!

Once you decide on a name, write it on paper and put it on your mirror or wall. Put it somewhere you will see it every day to remind yourself who you are now. The past will tug at you, but the more you interrupt this tug and refocus your attention on your Positive Bitch self, the easier it will be to embody that self.

Beliefs

The next step is our beliefs. What kind of beliefs does your Positive Bitch self have? What kind of beliefs have they let go of? Make two columns on a sheet of paper. On one side, write "My Positive Bitch Beliefs"; on the other side, write, "Faulty Programming." Write down all the beliefs you would have as your Positive Bitch self in one column and all the old programming beliefs you currently have in the other column.

Then rip this page in half, take the side with your Positive Bitch Beliefs, and put these statements somewhere you will see them every day. These are your new affirmations. Say these daily aloud.

Thoughts

The next step is our thoughts. What kinds of thoughts does your Positive Bitch self have? Thoughts of gratitude? Thoughts of service? Thoughts of starting that new business? What kind of thoughts does your current self have? What thoughts need to be let go of?

Again, make two columns on a sheet of paper. On one side, write "My Positive Bitch Thoughts," and on the other, "My Faulty Programming Thoughts." Write down all the thoughts you desire to have under your Positive Bitch Thoughts column, and all the current ones you wish to let go below your Faulty Programming side.

Then rip this page in half, take the side with your Positive Bitch thoughts, and put these statements somewhere you will see them every day. Anytime you feel yourself reverting to negative thoughts, use this list to INTERRUPT and reprogram yourself closer to your desired self.

Emotions

The next step is emotion. What kinds of emotions does your desired self feel? Happiness? Joy? Abundance? Pleasure? Practice feeling this emotion daily by focusing on something that already elicits that emotion within. When I am calling in more happiness, I play with my dogs, because they make me feel elevated. I have gratitude for what I already have because it makes me feel joy. I'll reflect on what I have accomplished, which makes me feel proud. If you have nothing to elicit these emotions, make a vision board of what would elicit those emotions and look to this vision board daily to inspire positive emotions within to be conjured up.

Actions

The next step is action. What kind of actions does your desired self do? Yoga? Walking? Charity? Side hustle? Write out all the actions of your Positive Bitch self, and then pick a few you can start immediately. Start signing up for classes or take whatever action you need to take to begin.

It's important to take action while you have the momentum and inspiration to do so. Don't wait. Once this list is made, take immediate action.

Habits

The next step is building actions into habits. What kinds of actions have turned into healthy habits? Breathwork? Meditation? Journaling? Write down all the habits of your Positive Bitch self, and start doing these immediately. If you need extra resources that you don't currently have, go out and get them! Practice these habits either daily or weekly.

250

Reality

Day after day, continue to show up as HER.

❤ ***This means before you think, act or speak, ask yourself, "Am I embodying my past self or my Positive Bitch self?"***

You must remind yourself every day to show up as who you wish to be. You must build this Positive Bitch self day after day to fully quantum-leap to that desired timeline. Read your affirmations daily, interrupt old faulty beliefs, practice your new preferred thoughts, break up with the low-vibe emotions, tune into higher-vibe emotions by envisioning what you want, do things that make you feel good, take those actions immediately, do it consistently, and there you have it, a transformed reality.

Practicing this one time is like dipping your toe into the pool. Practicing this every day consistently is like diving into this new reality. The more you practice, the more you are fine-tuning yourself and your point of attraction.

If you're feeling out of sorts or down on any given day, think of HER, your future desired self, and ask her to send you extra energy to stay on course on your way to your dream life. Remember, she already exists and can give you that extra boost of energetic encouragement when you need it: all you have to do is call on her. Close your eyes and feel her sending you white light energy right into your heart center. If you feel confused or not sure what steps to take, ask her, "What do you need me to do to get where you are?" Close your eyes and allow yourself to receive. The message from your future self may come in the form of an image, an idea, song lyrics, or a word. Don't limit the possibilities of how she will talk to you, just be open to receiving by clearing your mind and surrendering to her energy. On days you feel really good, think of your past self and send her love. You can do this by simply wishing her well, saying words of encouragement out loud, and/or sending her white light energy.

In case you're not exactly sure where to start with your new ego, I would like to leave you with my Self Laws, which you may wish to adopt too. This is what has allowed me to show up as my most Positive Bitch self.

251

Love thyself, and
others will love you too.

Value thyself, and
others will value you too.

Appreciate thyself, and
others will appreciate you too.

Respect thyself, and
others will respect you too.

Know thyself, and
others will want to know you too.

252

Trust thyself, and
others will trust you too.

Put yourself on your pedestal,
and others will look up to you.

How you treat yourself not only teaches others how to treat you, but it also teaches the Universe how to treat you. Create your own self laws and follow them. They will lead you back home to your pedestal.

Your New Life

I have impressed upon these words positive vibration and love. Just by reading this book, you have elevated your mindset and emotions, and therefore your overall energetic signature.

A congratu-fucking-lations is in order!

You have been triggered, you have been healing, and you have faced your old self, all while creating a bridge back home to your truest self.

While this book is finished, you are just beginning.

HOW EXCITING IS THAT?!

This book has provided you tools to align with your most Positive Bitch timeline.

You've always had the power.

Now it's time to anchor in the energy by practicing your new vibration with the tools you've been given.

Your most Positive Bitch timeline awaits your arrival, and I will see you there!

The sparkle in me honors the sparkle in you.

⟨ **Positive Bitch Tip:** Enjoy the fucking journey.

Acknowledgments

Thank you God and my spirit team for being my guiding light through every dark season. Even when I thought I was all alone, you have always been guiding me. Thank you to Mom and Dad for absolutely everything you've done for me, but most importantly for loving me and supporting me through every phase of my healing journey. I'm so happy I chose you as my parents during this incarnation. I love you both so much. Thank you to my boyfriend for being one of my greatest teachers and triggering my spiritual awakening. Without you, I wouldn't understand so much of myself and my purpose. There is no one else I would want to learn how to love and heal with. Thank you to my therapist, and to every shaman, reiki practitioner, and spiritual teacher that I've come into contact with. You all have been the perfect guide at the perfect time and have made a profound impact on my life. Thank you to all the Positive Bitches who saw a light in me before I saw it in myself and have been following me since the beginning of my TikTok, Instagram, and podcast, That Bitch is Positive. Thank you for trusting me as a guide on your journey. Thank you to all the new Positive Bitches who have picked up this book and connected with me now. I would like to lastly thank every past version of myself for never giving up and getting me here. Thank you.

About the Author

CiiCii is a vibrant and multi-talented creative force, inspiring millions around the world to reclaim their power and breathe life into their dreams. Her own journey, like that of many, was a meandering path filled with trials and transformations, which ultimately led her to align with her mission of empowering others on their own healing and spiritual journeys.

In her college years, CiiCii grappled with her weight, depression, anxiety, and a heart-wrenching breakup. Little did she know that this breakdown was ultimately the breakthrough of a lifetime. Learning to heal herself, she now empowers others to do the same.

CiiCii took her pain and transformed it into her purpose. She graduated summa cum laude from Fordham University with a double major in communications, studying TV/Film and Digital Technology/ Emerging Media. CiiCii embarked on a remarkable journey of online influence. She ventured into TikTok, sharing her spiritual awakening experiences and offering life-changing advice, amassing a dedicated following of over 400,000.

Driven by a deep desire to make a profoundly positive impact on the world, CiiCii expanded her mission by becoming a certified Life Coach through the prestigious Robbins-Madanes Training, led by Tony Robbins.

Today, as an in-demand life and energy coach, content creator, and podcaster, CiiCii's mission is rooted in creating transformative content that holds sacred space for individuals to heal and align with their most magnetic selves. Through her unique and empowering approach, she specializes in helping women become their very own Positive "B.I.T.C.H.," or Babe In True Connection with Herself. She skillfully translates the intricate languages of quantum physics, psychology, and spirituality into relatable, humorous talk, making these profound concepts easily digestible. Her teachings equip individuals to become their most confident and connected selves, guiding them through an array of spiritual practices, neurologically informed tools, and emotional exercises. Whether her words bring tears, laughter, or a profound sense of empowerment, they unfailingly leave you walking away as your most Positive Bitch self.

Connect with CiiCii:
Instagram: @vibinwithciicii
TikTok: @vibinwithciicii
Podcast: That Bitch is Positive

Mango Publishing, established in 2014, publishes an eclectic list of books by diverse authors—both new and established voices—on topics ranging from business, personal growth, women's empowerment, LGBTQ studies, health, and spirituality to history, popular culture, time management, decluttering, lifestyle, mental wellness, aging, and sustainable living. We were named 2019 *and* 2020's #1 fastest growing independent publisher by *Publishers Weekly*. Our success is driven by our main goal, which is to publish high-quality books that will entertain readers as well as make a positive difference in their lives.

Our readers are our most important resource; we value your input, suggestions, and ideas. We'd love to hear from you—after all, we are publishing books for you!

Please stay in touch with us and follow us at:

Facebook: Mango Publishing
Twitter: @MangoPublishing
Instagram: @MangoPublishing
LinkedIn: Mango Publishing
Pinterest: Mango Publishing
Newsletter: mangopublishinggroup.com/newsletter

Join us on Mango's journey to reinvent publishing, one book at a time.

Printed in the USA
CPSIA information can be obtained
at www.ICGtesting.com
JSHW030333050324
58476JS00004B/4

9 781684 811953